New Vanguard • 18

M2/M3 Bradley Infantry Fighting Vehicle 1983–95

Steven J Zaloga • Illustrated by Peter Sarson

First published in Great Britain in 1996 by Osprey Publishing,
Midland House, West Way, Botley, Oxford OX2 0PH, UK
44-02 23rd St, Suite 219, Long Island City, NY 11101, USA
E-mail: info@ospreypublishing.com

Transferred to digital print on demand 2007

First published 1996
4th impression 2005

Printed and bound by PrintOnDemand-Worldwide.com, Peterborough, UK

A CIP catalogue record for this book is available from the British Library

ISBN: 978 1 85532 538 8

Editing by Iain MacGregor
Index by Alan Rutter

Artist's Note
Readers may care to note the original paintings from which the colour plates in this book were
prepared are available for private sale. All reproduction copyright whatsoever is retained by the
publisher. All enquiries should be addressed to:

Appletree Cottage
211 Broadway Lane
Throop
Bournemouth
Dorset
BH8 0AE

The publishers regret that they can enter into no correspondence upon this matter.

Acknowledgements
The author would like to thank Mr R. William Highlander, communications director of United Defense
LP for his help in the supply of photographs and data used in this book. Thanks also go to Bob Lessels,
formerly with Aberdeen Proving Ground public affairs, Frank DeSisto, of the Intrepid Air-Land-Sea Museum,
Pierre Touzin, and Stephen 'Cookie' Sewell.

FOR A CATALOGUE OF ALL BOOKS PUBLISHED BY OSPREY
MILITARY AND AVIATION PLEASE CONTACT:

Osprey Direct, c/o Random House Distribution Center,
400 Hahn Road, Westminster, MD 21157
Email: uscustomerservice@ospreypublishing.com

Osprey Direct, The Book Service Ltd, Distribution Centre,
Colchester Road, Frating Green, Colchester, Essex, CO7 7DW
E-mail: customerservice@ospreypublishing.com

www.ospreypublishing.com

DESIGN AND DEVELOPMENT

By the 1950s, most major armies could agree about the general configuration of main battle tanks. But the same could not be said for armoured infantry vehicles. Several armies, including the US Army and the German Bundeswehr, adopted fully-tracked, fully-armoured vehicles such as the M59, the M113, and the HS.30. This type of infantry vehicle is often called an Armoured Personnel Carrier (APC), based on the common US terminology. In contrast, the Red Army adopted a mixture of wheeled transporters and tracked transporters such as the BTR-152 and BTR-60. Similarly, the British Army employed the Saracen and FV.432. Some of the vehicles, such as the German HS.30, were powerfully armed with a 20 mm cannon, while other vehicles had little more than a light machine gun (LMG). The reason for the variety of configurations was the rapidly evolving nature of mechanised infantry tactics and the relatively low priority afforded armoured infantry vehicles

compared to tanks. Even in the case of the Soviet and US armies, budget limitations led to the adoption of relatively simple and low cost armoured infantry transporters. In the 1960s, armoured infantry vehicles underwent the next major evolutionary step in the form of infantry combat vehicles, of which the Bradley was a relative latecomer. The reason for the US Army's decade of delay in adopting such a vehicle is a convoluted tale.

M113 APC

When the US Army's M113 Armoured Personnel Carrier appeared in 1959, it reflected the accepted American tactics of the day. The M113, like its predecessors, the M75 and M59 APCs, was an armoured 'battlefield taxi'. It would carry its squad to the battlefield, where the infantrymen would dismount from the vehicle to carry out their combat mission on foot. Although the M113 proved to be a durable and successful design, it came at a time when evolving infantry tactics raised serious questions about the 'battlefield taxi' idea. In the late 1950s, US Army doctrine in Europe came to rely increasingly on battlefield tactical nuclear weapons as a counterweight to the

The first attempt to field an infantry combat vehicle was the Pacific Car & Foundary XM701 MICV-65. The programme was shortlived due to the excessive weight of the prototype, as well as the enormous drain on research funds caused by the Vietnam War. (US Army)

The FMC Corp design, the XM723 MICV, was the forerunner of the current Bradley Fighting Vehicle. The hull configuration is very similar to the eventual Bradley design, but the one-man turret without an anti-tank missile launcher became the centre of dispute between the infantry and cavalry branches. (United Defense LP)

much larger Red Army. The US Congress was unwilling to fund conventional forces large enough to offer a credible deterrent, and so tactical nuclear weapons seemed to offer an economical alternative. There was a certain unreality to this doctrine and the NATO infantry tactics associated with it. If tactical nuclear weapons were to be used, it would be unrealistic to expect the APC's dismounted infantry to operate in radioactively contaminated areas.

BMP and Marder Projects
Both the German Bundeswehr and the Soviet Army were the first to tackle these two contradictory elements in contemporary battlefield doctrine. The Soviet Army decided to meet fire with fire: by the early 1960s it had deployed tactical nuclear artillery. With both sides contemplating the use of battlefield nuclear weapons, a radical revision of infantry tactics became increasingly urgent. Both the Soviet Army and the Bundeswehr concluded at roughly the same time that the solution was to allow the infantry to fight from within their armoured vehicles. This was an obvious and practical solution because the armoured shell of the vehicle already provided a measure of protection

from radiation, as well as the usual battlefield hazards (MG fire, artillery bursts, grenades, etc). In effect, the nuclear threat was forcing infantry to adopt tactics reminiscent of late 19th century cavalry. In addition, the vehicles could carry a heavy MG or other weapons to provide fire support for the infantry squad within. This reflected the general trend of increasing the firepower of infantry units, a process which began during the First World War.

The Soviet response to the nuclear battlefield was the BMP Infantry Combat Vehicle (ICV), which was first deployed in 1967. The German Bundeswehr followed two years later with their Marder ICV.

This new generation of infantry vehicles was far better armed than the previous generation: the BMP was fitted with a low-pressure 73 mm gun and an anti-tank missile launcher, while the Marder had a 20 mm auto-cannon. Both types could withstand heavy MG fire; this would have penetrated most earlier vehicles.

On the negative side, both the BMP and Marder carried a relatively small infantry squad compared to APCs such as the M113, since the weapon turret took up considerable space in the hull. The Marder had a crew of three plus a six-man dismountable squad; the BMP-1 had a crew of three and an eight-man dismountable squad. In comparison, the M113 had a crew of two and an 11-man dismountable squad. Traditional infantry officers were not happy with the abrupt drop in squad size. They were also dismayed by the technological complexity of these new ICVs, which tended to require almost as much attention as a main battle tank. Being comparatively simple, traditional APCs were much easier to maintain. Technological complexity also comes at a considerable cost. A typical APC cost about one-seventh to one-tenth the price of a contemporary tank, but a new generation IFV often cost half as much.

THE VIETNAM DETOUR

The US Army came to the same conclusion as the German and Soviet armies regarding the need for new mechanised infantry tactics. In March 1964 the US Army began accepting bids from US firms for the development of the new MICV-65

(Mechanized Infantry Combat Vehicle-1965). The Army finally selected the Pacific Car and Foundry design, designated the XM701, which was based around many components from the M109 and M110 families of self-propelled guns that the firm was manufacturing at the time. Testing of the XM701 was completed in 1966 but the design never proceeded to production. The Army concluded that the vehicle was too heavy (26-27 tons), could not be airlifted in a C-141 transport aircraft, and that it was too slow to keep up with forthcoming tanks such as the MBT-70. This was really only part of the problem. In fact, the Army was obliged to cut back on many of its ambitious new development programmes due to the rising cost of the war in Vietnam.

The Vietnam War helped kill the XM701 MICV-65 programme, but also strengthened Army interest in mounted infantry combat. In 1963 US Army advisors began teaching South Vietnamese troops traditional 'battlefield taxi' tactics using their new M113 APCs. The initial combat engagements of the South Vietnamese M113 units were debacles. The ARVN troops piled out their vehicles, and were mowed down by VC small arms fire. Not surprisingly, these tactics were dropped in favour of mounted attacks. The

The cancellation of the XM800 ARSV scout vehicle forced the re-design of the XM723 MICV turret. The US Army concluded that it could not afford a separate cavalry scout vehicle and infantry combat vehicle, and so merged both requirements into a single vehicle which emerged as the Bradley Fighting Vehicle. (Aberdeen Proving Ground)

VC, and later the NVA, were not particularly well equipped with anti-armour weapons, and mounted charges were often successful. The main problem with the use of the M113 in this fashion was that it had not been designed with such tactics in mind. Only a small portion of the squad could poke their heads out of the roof hatch to use their weapons. In so doing, they exposed themselves to small arms fire. An expedient solution was the M113 ACAV (armoured cavalry vehicle), which had armour shields added around the roof positions to counter small arms fire. There were also some experiments in the USA to modify the M113 by cutting side firing ports in the hull armour to permit the squad members inside to fire their weapons. Notable among these experiments was the XM734, some of which saw limited use in Vietnam. The real problem was that the M113 APC was not well configured for this role without serious redesign.

If Vietnam experience supported Army interest in mounted infantry tactics, it also drew attention to problems in APC design. All armoured troop transporters built during the 1960s were lightly armoured. This was due to two factors. On the one hand, 'battlefield taxi' tactics meant that such vehicles were not expected to encounter heavy anti-armour threats such as enemy tanks, anti-tank weapons or heavy anti-tank mines. They were only supposed to protect their passengers from overhead artillery airbursts, shrapnel, small arms and other anti-personnel weapons. But when used in mounted operations, they did encounter heavier weapons against which their armour was inadequate. An RPG-2 or RPG-7 rocket grenade, designed to cut through the heaviest tank armour, could easily penetrate an M113. More serious was the threat posed by large mines. An RPG's damage was usually limited to squad members in the narrow path of the spall cone; this usually meant that casualties were limited, unless a major internal fire or explosion resulted. In contrast, a large mine, designed to destroy a heavily armoured tank, could kill most of the squad inside an M113. Understandably, many squads took to riding on the outside of their M113s, fearing the deadly mine more than small arms fire.

Conditions in Vietnam were hardly identical to those in Central Europe. Mines were by far the greatest threat to armoured vehicles in Vietnam, while in a NATO environment direct-fire anti-armour weapons would play a much greater part.

Problems in Performance

The seemingly irrational desire to avoid the protection offered inside the M113 points to a major flaw in the 'battlefield taxi' concept. It ignores the psychological elements of mechanised infantry combat. APCs are not particularly comfortable to ride in, even in peacetime: a squad of 11 men is crammed into a space that is hardly the size of a small bathroom. It is too low for them to stand except at a crouch, and if the APC is fully manned the troops are packed so close together that they can hardly move their arms. Besides the infantrymen themselves, the insides are littered with their gear and weapons. In cross-country travel an APC offers a very jarring ride, aggravated by the fact that the occupants cannot see the terrain they are traversing, and so cannot anticipate jolts from terrain obstructions and ditches. APCs become unbearably hot in temperatures much above 75° F. When the hatches are all closed, there is only the pallid illumination of a small dome light, and the ventilation of a single fan.

The combination of cramped conditions, heat, diesel fumes, gloomy lighting; the confined stench of a squad of infantrymen in prolonged field conditions; and the nausea of a bouncing ride create a peculiar sort of claustrophobia. This mental tension only serves to worsen the infantryman's normal combat fears. Confined in a nauseating steel box, the soldier cannot see what fate awaits him outside – but he can hear the horrifying noise of battle over the din of a racing engine and the piercing creaks of the APC's tracks and suspension. A soldier who has seen combat knows what happens to the crew of an APC that runs over an anti-tank mine: its armour confines the mutilating blast of the mine inside the hull. Other threats are no less pleasant. Although an RPG might not wipe out a whole squad, an RPG hit throws a narrow spray of superheated gas and hyper-velocity metal shards into the vehicle. An infantryman sits with his back to the outside wall of the APC, where at any moment the fiery tongue of a RPG hit could enter. Even worse fates may be imagined should a tank fire on an APC with its main gun. A modern tank gun and some modern anti-tank guided missiles can ream out an APC with suitably horrific effects.

Not surprisingly, many infantrymen in combat would rather ride on the outside of an APC than

The series production M2 Bradley IFV differed in small details from the prototypes such as the configuration of the side firing ports. After a small number of vehicles were delivered in the multi-tone MERDC camouflage pattern in 1981, most subsequent Bradleys were delivered in a monotone forest green finish as seen here. (United Defense LP)

The merger of the infantry and cavlary requirements led to the addition of a TOW anti-tank missile on the vehicle. This dramatic view shows a BGM-71C Improved TOW shortly after launch with its two lateral rocket motor exhausts in full thrust. The TOW has undergone continuous evolution to keep up with advances in tank armour, and the Bradley A1 series was developed to take advantage of the BGM-71D TOW-2 missile. (Hughes Missile)

inside, even if the inside offers them protection against small arms, machine guns, artillery blasts and many other threats. With a head outside the confines of the APC, the claustrophobia is relieved: anxieties subside; horribly exaggerated fears shrink with a view of the battlefield. Very few battlefields are as horrible in reality as the imaginings of a frightened and anxious mind.

Most APCs have been designed against the objective threats of anti-personnel weapons; they have ignored the subjective threats to the morale of mechanised infantry posed by their armoured enclosure. There was growing recognition of this fact by armoured infantry vehicle designers in the late 1960s. A technical solution to the problem was to offer the enclosed crew a view outside the vehicle. This could relieve their anxieties, and partially compensate for some of the other prob-

lems of riding in an armoured vehicle. Moreover, such a feature coincided with the tactical requirements for a new generation of infantry combat vehicles which mandated firing ports to permit the infantry to fire their weapons from within the protected confines of the vehicle.

The MICV Testing

In 1968 the US Army formed a special task force headed by Maj. Gen. George Casey to re-examine whether an MICV was really needed. The Casey task force emphatically urged that the Army continue the development of an MICV. They pointed out not only that such a vehicle was necessary in order to permit infantry squads to operate in a contaminated environment or on a conventional battlefield, but also that important changes were occurring in Soviet infantry formations which mandated such a vehicle. The BMP had begun to appear; but this was only one small aspect of a dramatic Soviet Army programme to modernise its infantry. Besides the modest numbers of expensive BMPs being introduced, the Soviets were introducing large numbers of BTR-60 wheeled infantry transporters as part of a programme to replace conventional foot infantry in favour of a fully mechanised army. The US Army was being faced with the prospect that soon all Soviet divisions would be heavily equipped with both tanks and armoured troop transporters capable of destroying the M113. The M113s as not well enough armed to threaten any of these vehi-

The large hatch on the rear deck of the Bradley is used when reloading the TOW launcher. The hatch is designed to partially open, minimising the exposure of the crewman to hostile fire while reloading. (Author)

Like the M113 APC, the Bradley was designed to be amphibious. However, its greater weight forced the use of a swimming screen, similar to that first used on the DD Sherman tanks during the Normandy campaign in June 1944. There were early problems with the screen which sometimes collapsed if the vehicle was driven too quickly into the water. Propulsion in the water is accomplished using the tracks. (Pierre Touzin)

cles. As a result, a new MICV project manager's office was opened in 1968.

FMC Corporation, the manufacturer of the highly successful M113 APC, had been one of the losing bidders on the MICV-65 programme. Although the M113 was still in production, company officials realised that the future of the APC business was moving in the direction of new gen-

eration of ICVs. Using their own funds, the company redesigned the M113 as an IFV called the XM765 AIFV (Armored Infantry Fighting Vehicle), and tried to interest the Army in it. In 1969 and 1970, the MICV Office examined this option, as well as considering whether the US Army might adopt the German Marder to satisfy its MICV requirement. The XM765 AIFV was rejected by the Army as an unsatisfactory half-way measure. At the time, the new M1 Abrams tank was in development, and the Army was insistent that a new MICV be as fast and mobile as the new tank. In addition, the Army wanted more armour protection while the XM765 was little better protected than the older M113 APC.

As a result, in November 1972, the Army awarded FMC Corp. a contract to develop a vehicle similar to the XM765 AIFV, but faster and better armoured. This vehicle was the XM723 MICV (Mechanized Infantry Combat Vehicle). The MICV closely resembled the AIFV, but was based on heavier components derived from the LVTP-7 Marine Corps Amtrac rather than the lighter M113. The technical requirements for the vehicle were not particularly exotic. The MICV was to be armed with a 20 mm gun in a small one-man turret, with firing ports for its nine-man squad. It was to be protected by a novel laminated

This is the view looking from the troop compartment up into the Bradley turret. The gunner sits at the left, and operates the 25 mm gun. The breech of the M242 25 mm Bushmaster gun is enclosed behind the panel visible in the centre. The vehicle commander sits on the right hand side of the turret. (Author)

The only major exterior detail distinguishing the M2 IFV from the M3 CFV was the firing port. This is a firing port on a M2 IFV without the firing port weapon attached. (Author)

The firing port on the M3CFV was blanked off since the space behind the port was taken up by storage. On later production M3 CFV vehicles, the entire firing port area was faired over. (Author)

steel/aluminium armour developed by FMC, which was relatively light in weight but offered greatly improved protection against small projectiles of up to 14.5 mm calibre. It was capable of speeds up to 45 mph.

Although the technical requirements for the new MICV were not overly complicated, its fate soon became entangled with other programmes that would eventually delay its development. The armament selected for the MICV was the VRFWS-S, a new externally powered autocannon. Prolonged problems with the VRFWS-S forced the Army to consider using the older M139 20 mm cannon but these guns differed so much that it would have forced time-consuming changes in turret configuration.

The ARSV Project

Far more troublesome was the interference of the Army's new cavalry scout vehicle. The XM800 ARSV programme originated in October 1971, when Lockheed and FMC were given competitive development contracts for the design of a new Armoured Reconnaissance Scout Vehicle. The winner of the ARSV competition was intended to replace the troubled M114 and M551 Sheridan cavalry scout vehicles. Government tests began in

November 1973 and FMC's XM800-T tracked ARSV was impressive. However, the programme came under fire from US Army Training and Doctrine Command (TRADOC). The programme was not challenged on the grounds of the technical requirements of the design, nor on the basis of the need for a new scout vehicle. Rather, the Army was coming to realise that in the wake of Vietnam, the Congress was not very enthusiastic about funding a host of new Army programmes. In the early 1970s, the Army had an expensive array of new programmes which had been postponed or cancelled due to the costs of the Vietnam war: a new helicopter to replace the UH-1 Huey; a new attack helicopter to replace the AH-1 Cobra and the cancelled AH-56 Cheyenne; a new main battle tank to replace the M60 and cancelled MBT-70; a new armoured infantry vehicle to replace the M113 and the cancelled XM701 MICV-65; a new mobile air defence gun to replace the interim M163 Vulcan; and a new mobile air defence missile vehicle to replace the interim M48 Chaparral system. All this added up to a considerable amount of money. The situation was not helped by the anti-military mood in Congress over the recent Vietnam quagmire, and this mood was further worsened by the widespread perception in Congress that many of the Army's weapons designs in the 1960s had been a bit too gold-plated and unnecessarily complicated.

The cancellation of the XM800 ARSV programme in November 1974 was indicative of an Army recognition of the political and fiscal realities of future Army budgets in Congress. The idea to merge the ARSV and MICV into a common vehicle emerged in early 1975. TRADOC concluded that a scout version of the MICV would need some anti-tank capability, and that a two-man turret would be superior to the XM723's one-man turret, since it would allow the second crewman to act as an observer. As the ARSV requirement was being examined, US Army intelligence was beginning to pick up signs of major policy debates in the Soviet Army over the BMP infantry combat vehicle.

There was lingering controversy within the Soviet Army over the high cost of the BMP, as well as from concern that the BMP was not as well suited to a non-nuclear battlefield as to a nuclear one.

US intelligence reports on the Soviet contro-

The infantry squad in the M2 Bradley CFV were armed with the M231 5.56 mm Firing Port Weapon while fighting from within the vehicle. This was a modified version of the M16A1 assault rifle, fitted with a special adaptor for attachment to the firing port, and engineered to fire only at full automatic. On disembarking, the infantryman was armed with a second weapon, usually a M16 assault rifle. (Author)

versy prompted the Secretary of the Army to challenge the basic MICV concept. This resulted in the establishment of yet another special task force, this time headed by Brig. Gen. Larkin. The Larkin Task Force examined three issues. Was the XM723 the right vehicle, or were foreign alternatives more suitable? Was the basic notion of an MICV sound? How could the MICV and ARSV requirements best be harmonised into a single vehicle?

The Army again examined foreign alternatives to see if they would be more cost-effective. The Marder was very popular with US Army officers familiar with it from tours of duty in Germany. However, as in the case of the first task force, it was turned down due to its high cost, its heavy weight and lack of amphibious capabilities, its relatively light armour, and its armament system. The MICV requirement called for protection against at least 14.5 mm cannons like that on the BTR-60PB, and the preferred armament solution was a heavier gun with full stabilisation to permit firing while on the move. The French AMX-10 was also examined and rejected, and the task force examined some BMP-1s captured by the Israelis from the Syrians.

Heavy infantry vehicles?
The task force accepted that the XM723 MICV was not adequately armoured to protect it against all anti-tank weapons but recognised that its tactical employment could help minimise exposure to

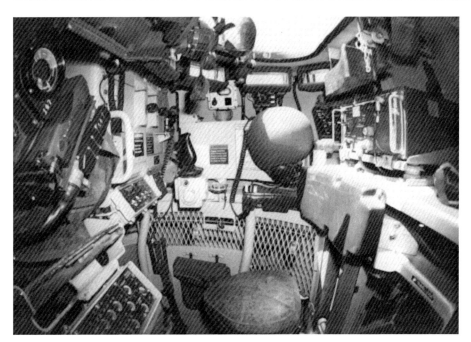

This is a view of the turret from the gunner's side of the turret, looking over to the commander's station on the right hand side. The rear bustle of the turret contains the vehicle radios. While riding inside the Bradley, the commander wears a normal CVC helmet which is attached to the vehicle's communication system. (Author)

The left hand interior of the M2 Bradley IFV has stowage for four TOW or Dragon anti-tank missiles. This places them within easy reach of the crewman in the left rear of the troop compartment for reloading the TOW launcher. (Author)

The right hand side of the M2 IFV troop compartment contains seating for four of the squad's infantrymen, as well as a variety of stowage. The firing ports for the M231 FPWs are somewhat obscured in this view by stowage, but can be detected under the two periscopes with careful attention. (Author)

such weapons. This was not an ideal solution: inevitably, MICVs would encounter such weapons on the battlefield. But realistically, there were no alternatives. As the result of pressure in the Army from advocates of an MICV as heavily armoured as a tank, a separate study was conducted of the 'Tank Infantry Vehicle' notion. Even if refurbished M48 hulls were used as an economy measure, such a vehicle would cost twice as much as the MICV.

This conclusion was hardly unique to the US Army. No army to date has adopted an armoured infantry transporter as heavily armoured as a tank except on an expedient basis. In World War 2, the British Army used 'Ram Kangaroos' which were based on obsolete Ram tank hulls; and the Israelis have made limited use of small numbers of Centurion and T-55 hulls. The problem is quite simply that such vehicles are too expensive. The cost of the added armour is not the main problem: but more armour means extra weight, thereby requiring a more powerful (and expensive) engine, transmission, suspension, and other components. Heavier vehicles increase wear on tracks and other components. A heavy infantry vehicle not only costs twice as much as an MICV, but its lifetime support costs are also considerably higher. US sources estimate that the lifetime costs of a tank-

like armoured vehicle are four times the basic purchase price over a 20-year period due to the higher level of wear on the powertrain and suspension. Light armoured vehicles do not have such a high lifetime cost relative to their purchase price due to the lesser strain they place on running gear and engines. Most armies buy more armoured infantry transporters than tanks, and none has been able so far to enjoy the luxury of a heavy infantry vehicle. Besides the cost problems, there are tactical drawbacks as well. A heavy infantry vehicle cannot be made amphibious, requiring an army to expand its stockpile of tactical bridging for river crossing operations. For the US Army, weight is a serious drawback, since in an emergency vehicles have to be shipped or airlifted great distances.

There is no happy middle ground in this controversy. On the modern battlefield, weapons tend to congregate in two broad categories. Antipersonnel weapons are the most numerous, and are countered by light armour as on the MICV. At the other end of the spectrum are the antiarmour weapons. Even relatively small weapons like the RPG-7 have phenomenal penetration performance. The RPG-7 can penetrate 13 in. of steel, and more modern types can penetrate up to 16 in.– equivalent to battleship armour. Due to the nature of army weapons, armour configurations are either on the light side (to defend against anti-personnel weapons) or extremely heavy and tank-like (to defend against anti-tank weapons). There is little sense in adopting an armour level in between.

In November 1976 the Larkin Task Force concluded in favour of the MICV concept, as well as the case for merging the MICV and the ARSV requirements. They agreed with the cavalry advocates, who wanted a two-man turret, armed with a TOW anti-tank missile launcher.

BRADLEY DEVELOPMENT BEGINS

The new XM723 derivative was designated the XM2 Infantry Fighting Vehicle (IFV) for the MICV requirement, and the XM3 Cavalry Fighting Vehicle (CFV) to satisfy the ARSV requirement. Not unexpectedly, the XM2/XM3 Fighting Vehicle System (FVS) proceeded relatively smoothly. Problems with the transmission

on the XM723 led to a competitive development programme, with General Electric receiving the nod in June 1977. The decision to adopt a two-man turret caused some controversy in the infantry. The two man turret inevitably cut into the size of the squad that could be carried, lowering the total crew size from 11 to nine, and the squad size from nine to seven. This had its advantages. The turret offered a better station for the squad leader, giving him better control over the vehicle, especially its weapons. The added twin TOW anti-tank missile launcher subsequently won the enthusiastic endorsement of the infantry units who began receiving the M2 in 1982. Thanks to the TOW launcher, infantry squads know that they are not helpless if confronted by tanks – as is unfortunately the case with the M113.

M2 IFV & M3 CFV

In 1978 the initial eight prototypes were delivered for testing, which proceeded without any major difficulties. In January 1980 the Secretary of Defense gave production approval. Following type classification, they became the M2 IFV and M3 CFV. Although there were originally plans to name the M2 after Gen. Omar Bradley, and the M3 after Gen. Jacob Devers, the two famous World War Two commanders, it was eventually

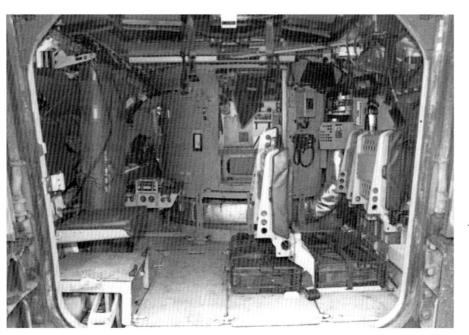

Studies of the high-survivability Bradley led to some reconfiguration of the troop compartment in the M2A2 IFV, notably the new arrangement of the two squad seats on the extreme right side due to the deletion of the firing ports. There have also been some layout changes in ammunition. One of the most important changes, the addition of Kevlar spall liners, is not readily evident from the photo. (Author)

The M3 CFV has a signficantly different configuration of stowage in the back due to the smaller squad size. The two rear jump seats for the dismount team face backward so that the scouts can use the rear firing ports. The right sponson is full of BGM-71 TOW missiles. (Author)

decided to name them both after Gen. Bradley due to the basic similarity of the vehicles. The US Army is overly fond of acronyms, and so the IFV and CFV received a collective acronym, the BFV (Bradley Fighting Vehicle), which shows up regularly in official Army descriptions of the vehicle. Funding for the first 100 Bradleys was provided in the Fiscal Year (FY) 1980 budget, consisting of 75 M2 IFV and 25 M3 CFV. This was followed by 400 more in FY81, then 600 annually until 1984, rising to 680 in FY85. The first Bradleys were delivered in May 1981. By 1982 enough had been produced to begin equipping mechanised infantry units, with the 41st Infantry, 2nd Armored Division at Ft. Hood being the first. In 1983 the first Bradleys were delivered to Europe, equipping the 3rd Infantry Division (Mechanised).

Criticisms of project
Although the Bradley had passed its technical and operational tests without difficulty, it was subjected to prolonged media bashing in 1983-84. Further fuel was thrown on the Bradley controversy in 1984 as a result of charges that aluminium armour amplified the effects of shaped-charge impact. The critics were apparently unaware that several countries including the US had used aluminium armoured vehicles in combat

without encountering such effects. The M2 Bradley was labelled a 'death trap' and a 'crematorium' in the newspapers and weekly magazines, and the Army brass was castigated for its 'callous disregard' for the safety of its troops. The fact that the Bradley is more heavily armoured than any other infantry vehicle in production was ignored. Nor did any of its critics suggest they would support a programme for a heavy infantry vehicle with all its attendant higher costs. The top Army leadership placed a high priority on the Bradley programme, and as a result, the Press failed to derail it. Operation 'Desert Storm' refuted the critics.

Inside the Bradley
The M2 IFV and M3 CFV are almost identical externally; they differ mainly internally. The main external differences are the absence of firing port periscopes on the right side and the plating-over of firing ports on the M3. Internally, the main differences are in the rear troop compartment. The M2, being a squad carrier, has seating for six to seven men (in addition to the driver, gunner and squad/vehicle leader in the turret). In contrast, the M3 CFV carries only two men in the rear. Some thought was given to using the additional space in the M3 to carry a scout motorcy-

This view of the left side of the M3 CFV troop compartment shows the large stowage racks for 25 mm ammunition containers in the sponson. The large black plastic magazines contain 30 rounds of 25 mm ammunition. (Author)

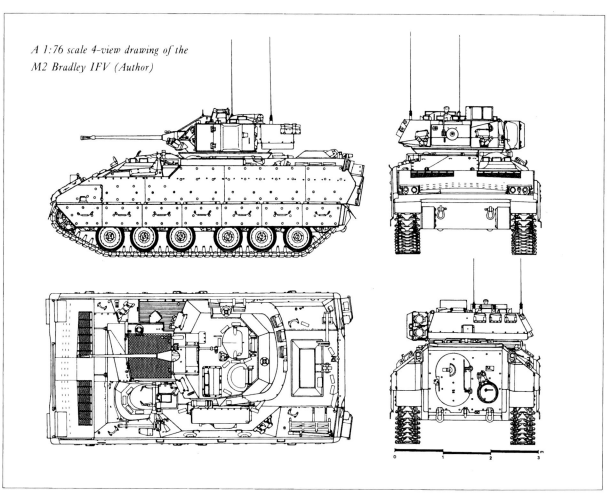

A 1:76 scale 4-view drawing of the M2 Bradley IFV (Author)

cle. This idea was eventually dropped due to the hazard presented by the motorcycle's unprotected gasoline tank in such a confined space. Instead, the M3 is configured to carry additional rounds of TOW anti-tank missiles and other munitions.

M2 IFV

The M2 IFV is configured differently from either the German Marder or the Soviet BMP. Like both these earlier vehicles, it has its engine up front, with the driver to the left. The placement of the engine and transmission provide a certain measure of additional protection to the turret and rear crew positions in the event of a hit on the hull front. The driver is provided with a hydrostatic steering system which is quite simple to operate and incorporates a 'butterfly' steering yoke. Behind the driver and engine are the turret and squad positions. Since the turret is offset to the right, there is a tunnel between the driver's station and the rear crew compartment. Two of the squad sit in the tunnel, and operate the two left side M231 Firing Port Weapons (FPW). (The FPW is a sub-machine gun version of the M16A1 assault rifle, configured to fire only on automatic, with special tracer ammunition to assist in aiming.)

The decision to adopt a firing port weapon in lieu of using an unmodified MI6AI was due to the length of the M16A1 and the difficulty of designing a firing port sufficiently secure to permit the use of a CBR (Chemical/Biological/Radiation) system. This has meant that each squad member has both a FPW while on board the IFV, and his regular weapon: either an unmodified M16, or another squad weapon such as the M249 SAW (Squad Automatic Weapon) when dismounted.

There has been some question as to the effectiveness of the firing port weapon concept, not only on the Bradley but on the Marder and BMP as well. The weapon is aimed using a periscope mounted above the firing port. The weapon can only be aimed by adjusting fire after observing the fall of the tracer, since the normal sight cannot be used. This hardly results in sharpshooting. For

The first unit equipped with the M2 Bradley IFV was the 41st Infantry (Mechanized), 2nd Armoured Division at Ft. Hood, Texas, which began receiving the vehicles in 1982. These vehicles from the initial production run still have the four-colour MERDC camouflage pattern, and on the hull side is the black triangle used at the time by the 2nd Armoured Division to distinguish its vehicles from those of the neighbouring 1st Cavalry Division. (Author)

The first deployment of Bradleys to Europe began in 1983 and they soon became a familiar sight at the autumn Reforger wargames. This Bradley has been decorated with pine boughs. From this view, it is impossible to distinguish whether it is a M2 IFV or M3 CFV as the firing ports are covered. (Pierre Touzin)

this reason, FPW fire is usually referred to as 'suppressive': that is, it is not accurate enough for precision, but may intimidate the enemy and force him to keep his head down.

The rear squad compartment contains the remaining four members of the squad. Two are seated so as to use the two right side firing ports, and two by the rear firing ports. The rear area also contains additional 25 mm main gun ammunition stowage and further TOW missile rounds. The TOW 'twin pack' launcher on the turret carries two rounds. Once these are expended, the launcher is reloaded by one of the squad members in the rear compartment using the rear roof hatch. The hatch is designed to be partly opened, giving the crewman complete overhead protection during reloading, as well as minimising his exposure to hostile fire. Access to the troop compartment is through the large rear drop ramp, or through the door in the ramp itself. The upper hull hatch is not intended for access or egress.

The turret is in the centre of the Bradley, offset to the right. It is armed with an M242 25 mm Bushmaster externally-powered Chain Gun, a co-axial M240 machine gun, smoke dischargers, and an elevatable twin TOW launcher. The turret is occupied by the squad/vehicle leader on the right and the gunner on the left. The squad leader has 360-degree vision periscopes. In addition, he is provided with a special hatch that can be locked above his head, permitting him to look outside the vehicle without using the periscopes, while at the same time offering total overhead armour coverage from shell bursts. All weapon controls are duplicated at both the commander's and gunner's stations, allowing either crewman to engage targets as necessary. Due to this feature, either member of the turret crew may disembark with the remainder of the squad to bolster their numbers if need be. The main advantage of this configuration is that, unlike the BMP-1 or Marder, it provides the squad leader with a good view all around the battlefield. Furthermore, he is not as isolated from his squad as is the case in the BMP or Marder.

The weapons are aimed using an Integrated Sight Unit (ISU), which incorporates both a daylight mode and a thermal imaging night system. The thermal imaging sight may also be used during the day to see through clouds of dust, smoke or haze. This can have a tactical advantage, since a Bradley can produce its own smoke screen and then target an enemy vehicle from within it. This advantage comes at a price: the ISU represents about a tenth of the total vehicle cost. The M242 Bushmaster cannon is fully stabilised, enabling the vehicle to fire on the move. Either a high or low rate of fire may be selected, the high rate being 200 rounds per minute. Normally, the gun is fired in bursts of four to six rounds, since keeping your finger on the trigger can lead to greater round dis-

persion at long ranges. The usual mix of ammunition in the ready magazine is 75 rounds of armour piercing (AP), and 225 rounds of high explosive (HE). A further 600 rounds is stowed in the vehicle. The Bradley initially used the M791 armour piercing discarding sabot (APDS), projectile with a tungsten carbide core, and the improved M919 depleted uranium, fin-stabilised projectile became available in limited quantities in 1991. The M919 is apparently able to penetrate over 30 mm of armour at 60 degrees/2000 metres, enough to take out virtually any armoured infantry vehicle at normal combat ranges, and defeat the side and rear armour of some tanks. To deal with tanks frontally, the Bradley has the twin TOW launcher. This is elevated for firing, and the missile controls are integrated into the ISU day/night sight to permit operation under nearly all conditions. The launcher is not designed to be used while moving at normal speeds, and is generally retracted at more than 5 km/h. The initial M2 IFV can fire TOW and Improved TOW missiles.

M3 CFV

The M3 CFV is nearly identical to the M2, except for the rear compartment. The internal stowage on this version is different, accommodating more ammunition. The turret weapon system is identical in all respects. The Bradley is amphibious after preparation. A flotation screen is contained along the hull sides, and is erected prior to entering the water.

The Bradley is powered through the water using its tracks, and can be 'swum' across rivers and lakes without strong current or wave action. Constraints on its swimming are similar to those for most other amphibious armoured vehicles except for 'dedicated' amphibians like the LVT-7 amtracs. Through 1987, the US Army had conducted about 10,000 swimming exercises, but had problems in 13 cases: most often a collapsed swim vane that led to the vehicle sinking.

The Bradley employs a mixture of steel and aluminium alloy armour. The basic hull structure is No. 5083 aluminium armour plate, an alloy containing zinc and magnesium. Aluminium is an attractive option in light armoured vehicles since for a given weight, it is structurally stiffer than a comparable steel structure, lessening the overall weight of the vehicle by obviating the need for stiffners and reinforcement. Some of the side slopes of the vehicle use No. 7039 aluminium armour, which is better suited to defeating armour piercing ammunition. The vertical hull sides have

An M3 CFV of the 1st Cavalry Division during exercises at Ft. Hood Texas in 1987. During the production of the Bradley, a continual series of small improvements were added to the vehicle, such as the guard placed at the base of the turret radio antenna to prevent it from being broken by crewmen climbing into the turret. The crews at some posts operate the Bradley with the lower skirt raised since it eases track maintenance. In the case of this Bradley, the vehicle tactical number, 112, has been added on the inside of the skirt in reflective tape. (Author)

a pair of laminated 25 mm high-hardness steel plates spaced one inch from one another and 3.5 inches from the base aluminium armour.

Mechanised Infantry Organisation

The Bradley was developed concurrently with the US Army's new Division 86 organisation and doctrine. The new 'Div 86' heavy divisions are equipped with the M1 Abrams tank and M2 IFV in lieu of the older M60A3 tank and M113 APC. The Div 86 follows the new H-series TOE (table of organisation and equipment) as compared to the J-series TOE used with M113 battalions. It is worth comparing the two mechanised infantry battalions, as they serve to place the capabilities of the Bradley in better focus.

Under the H-series TOE, a Bradley mechanised infantry battalion has four rifle companies, instead of the three companies in a J-series TOE for an M113 battalion. There are 13 Bradleys in each rifle company, organised into three platoons of four vehicles each and a company commander's vehicle. This gives the battalion a total of 54 M2 IFVs (counting the battalion commander's and the S3's vehicles). The other change from the M113 battalion has been the amalgamation of the combat support company into the headquarters company,

and the creation of an anti-tank company using the battalion's 12 M901 ITV tank destroyers. The battalion support platoon has additional fuel- and ammunition-hauling capability, with more trucks and trailers. Other armour in the new battalion includes six M3 CFVs in the battalion headquarters company, as well as six M106 4.2 in. self-propelled mortars (based on the M113 chassis). These new weapons give the battalion considerably more firepower than previously. The J-series TOW M113 battalion has only 22 long-range anti-armour weapons consisting of TOW's and M901 ITV tank destroyers: in contrast, the new H-series TOE M2 battalion has 72. When the wealth of 25 mm guns are factored in, the new battalion has 132 long-range anti-armour weapons.

The firepower of each platoon is equally impressive, even though the Bradley squads are smaller than the old M113 squad. In each platoon, three rifle squads are formed from the four Bradleys. Each Bradley retains a 'fighting vehicle team', consisting of the driver, gunner, and either the assistant squad leader or the squad leader. Each of the three squads consists of a squad leader (or assistant squad leader), armed with an M16A2; a machine gunner (M60 7.62 mm machine gun); an anti-armour specialist (Dragon anti-tank missile, Javelin in the future); two automatic riflemen (each with an M249 SAW); a grenadier (M16A2 with M203 40 mm grenade launcher); and a radio operator armed with an M16A2. Normally, three M72A2 LAW or AT-4 anti-armour rockets are also carried by the squad. Currently, the platoon has no organic anti-aircraft weapon comparable to the Strela-2/Igla (SA-7/SA-16) carried in the Russian BMP. However, as in the Russian case, anti-aircraft resources could be shared out below battalion level if and when required. In any event, the 25 mm gun on the M2 can be used against helicopters.

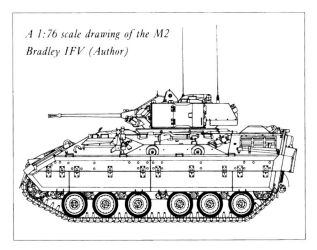

A 1:76 scale drawing of the M2 Bradley IFV (Author)

THE BRADLEY COMPARED

The M2 Bradley is more comparable to the newer Soviet BMP-2 than to the original BMP-1. Not unnaturally, the BMP-2 evolved from the BMP-1, from which it differs mainly in having a new, larger, two-man turret with a 30 mm auto-cannon in lieu of the older 73 mm low pressure gun. In this respect the Russians have been paralleling US IFV development.

In the area of firepower, the Bradley has some advantage due to better ammunition. The 25 mm Bushmaster can penetrate about 33 mm at 60 degrees at 1 km, and 28 mm at 2 km using the M791 APDS round; the Russian 30 mm 2A42 gun can penetrate about 20 mm at 1.5 km. The Bradley carries 900 rounds of ammunition vs. 500 on the BMP-2; and seven missiles vs. six due to

A column of M2A1 Bradleys of the 2nd Armoured Cavalry passes though a small Bavarian town during the January 1990 'Reforger' exercise. Bradley A1 variant had numerous internal changes including alterations to permit the use of

the improved TOW-2 missile and upgrades in the chemical protection system. One of the few external manifestations of this version is the absence of a fixed smoke grenade box on the face of the turret. (Author)

A M3A1 CFV leads a column of M1 Abrams tanks during a field exercise in Germany in 1989. A careful inspection of the side plate below the TOW launcher will reveal the absence of firing ports on this vehicle, a sure sign that it is a Cavalry Fighting Vehicle. (Pierre Touzin)

its greater internal volume. The BMP-2 suffers in comparison to the M2 IFV in terms of weapons stabilisation, fire control and ammunition stowage. The BMP-2 is not regularly equipped with a thermal imaging night sight and is limited to image intensification sights, which can only be used when there is adequate ambient moonlight. These systems have no capability to peer through haze, dust or smoke in daylight as the Bradley's ISU can. In terms of anti-tank missiles, the TOW-1 on the Bradley and 9M113 Konkurs on the BMP-2 are similar in performance. The later TOW-2A and TOW-2B are claimed to have a number of advantages over the latest versions of the Konkurs, particularly against tanks protected by advanced armours.

The BMP-1 was already badly cramped; the BMP-2, with its larger turret, is even worse, habitability being particularly poor. Although the M2 could hardly be described as spacious, it is considerably better than the BMP in this respect. While this feature may seem a luxury, excessively cramped spaces add to crew fatigue and can degrade squad performance in prolonged combat actions. This became very evident during Soviet operations in Afghanistan when the BMP-2 required so much exterior stowage that the turret could not traverse to the rear. Although the Bradley also needed exterior stowage during

'Desert Storm', its location did not interfere with the performance of the vehicle.

The armour of the BMP-2 is similar to that on the BMP-1, meaning that it can be penetrated at nearly any angle by the 25 mm gun on the M2 at normal combat ranges. The armour on the baseline Bradley A0 cannot protect it against the BMP's 30 mm autocannon but the upgraded armour on the Bradley A2 is probably resistent to 30 mm fire.

Russia's latest infantry vehicle is the BMP-3, a radical departure in terms of firepower with a 100 mm low-pressure gun and a co-axial 30 mm cannon. It is not clear if this represents the direction of future Russian IFV development. Although exceedingly well armed, the troop compartment in the BMP-3 is poorly configured for troop access and armour protection is little better than the BMP-2. After combat experience in Chechnya in 1995, there has been talk of a BMP-4 with armament reverting to a single 30 mm gun, but with greater armour protection.

Interestingly enough, a Russian assessment of infantry vehicle combat potential agrees that the M2 Bradley has advantages over the BMP-2. In 1991, they released a previously classified assessment of the combat potential of various contemporary armoured infantry vehicles. One vehicle (the Italian VCC-80) was selected as the baseline and given a value of 1.0, while all other vehicles were judged against it, numbers over 1.0 indicating the percentage advantage. The new British Warrior was given a relatively low rating due to its lack of an anti-tank missile system, though its 'inferiority' to the BMP-1 or BMP-2 is, to say the least, debatable.

IFV Combat Potential Table

BMP-3 (Russia)	1.73
M2A1 Bradley IFV (US)	1.29
BMP-2 (Russia)	1.22
BMP-1 (Russia)	1.09
Marder 1 (Germany)	1.09
Warrior (UK)	1.03
AMX-10P (France)	0.85
BTR-80 APC (Russia)	0.62
M113A1 APC (USA)	0.59

MODERNISATION

The Bradley was developed from the outset to permit modular 'Block' improvements. The first series of improvements were the M2E1 and M3E1 which became the M2A1 and M3A1 when accepted. The principal modification involves the chemical protection system and the TOW launcher. The baseline Bradley (now called A0) has no integral chemical defence system, and the

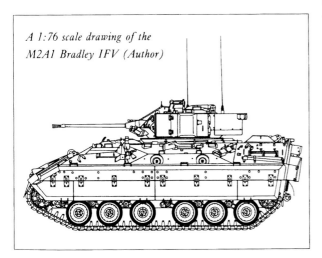

A 1:76 scale drawing of the M2A1 Bradley IFV (Author)

squad must wear their suits for chemical protection. The next generation Bradley A1 incorporates a Gas Particulate Filter Unit (GPFU): this provides purified air to the entire vehicle crew (through their M24/M25 masks) in the M3A1, and to the turret crew and driver in the M2A1. The other squad members in the M2A1 continue to use their own filter units. The US Army is reluctant to incorporate a full overpressure system into the M2 such as that used in the BMP: the feeling is that in chemical battlefield conditions, the system would be quickly compromised by the squad mounting and dismounting from the vehicle. The Soviet system appears to have been developed mainly for use in nuclear battlefield conditions, where the squad would remain aboard the vehicle for prolonged periods.

The other main change involves adaption of the TOW launcher to permit it to fire the BGM-71D TOW-2 missile with its improved warhead. The new version was capable of defeating any existing Soviet tank head-on through the use of an increased diameter (6 in.) warhead. There are also many other small changes in the pipeline. In the M2A1 these mainly concern internal stowage improvements. External changes on the M3A1 include removal of the vestigial closed firing ports and periscope cut-out in favour of continuous armour; a new rear hatch with periscopes to permit improved rear squad vision; and many internal stowage changes. Production of the resulting M2A1 and M3A1 Bradleys began in May 1986 with the TOW-2 features being phased in during early 1987; these features were later retro-fitted to the initial production vehicles.

The appearance of the Soviet BMP-2 infantry fighting vehicle and the criticism directed against the Bradley regarding its armour protection led to a programme in 1984 to develop a High Survivability Version (HSV) which eventually emerged in May 1988 as the M2A2 and M3A2 Bradley. The most obvious change in this version is the addition of large panels of appliqué steel armour to the hull and turret. In addition, Kevlar fabric armour spall liners were added over key locations inside the hull to minimise casualties in the event of hull penetration by trapping small fragments of metal (spall) before they can enter

The appearance of the Soviet BMP-2 led to the High Survivability Vehicle programme in 1984, culminating in the M2A2 Bradley IFV. The most obvious change introduced on this version was additional appliqué armour added to the front and sides. This is a vehicle of Delta Company, 3-15th Infantry, 24th Infantry Division (Mech) at Ft. Stewart, Georgia in 1992. This division still was equipped with older M2 and M2A1 Bradleys during 'Desert Storm', but re-equipped after the war. The vehicles remain in the CARC tan camouflage since the division is part of the US Army's rapid reaction force. The V on the turret is the divisional insignia ('Victory Division') while the black triangle is the D Company insignia. (Author)

the crew compartment. The high survivability version was also designed from the outset to accept an additional layer of reactive armour tiles to further protect the vehicle against large calibre shaped charge warheads, such as those from anti-tank guided missiles. Although attachments for these tiles were incorporated at the outset, the US Army did not begin to order a production config-

uration tile until October 1993, when a team of Martin Marietta (now Lockheed Martin) and Israel's Rafael development agency were given an award for a pre-production test batch.

The additional armour led to the deletion of most of the firing ports in the rear compartment of the IFV; the only two remaining are on the back cargo door. There was also some reorganisa-

Bradley Production Figures

PROCUREMENT FUNDING

Fiscal year & Quantity

FY80	FY81	FY82	FY83	FY84	FY85	FY86	FY87	FY88	FY89	FY90	FY91	FY92	FY93	FY94
100	400	600	600	600	655	716	662	554	644	400	300	300	200	54

Production breakdown: M2 IFV = 4,641 M3 CFV = 2,083 Total = 6,724
Initial configuration: A0= 2,300 A1= 1,371 A2 = 3,053 Total = 6,724

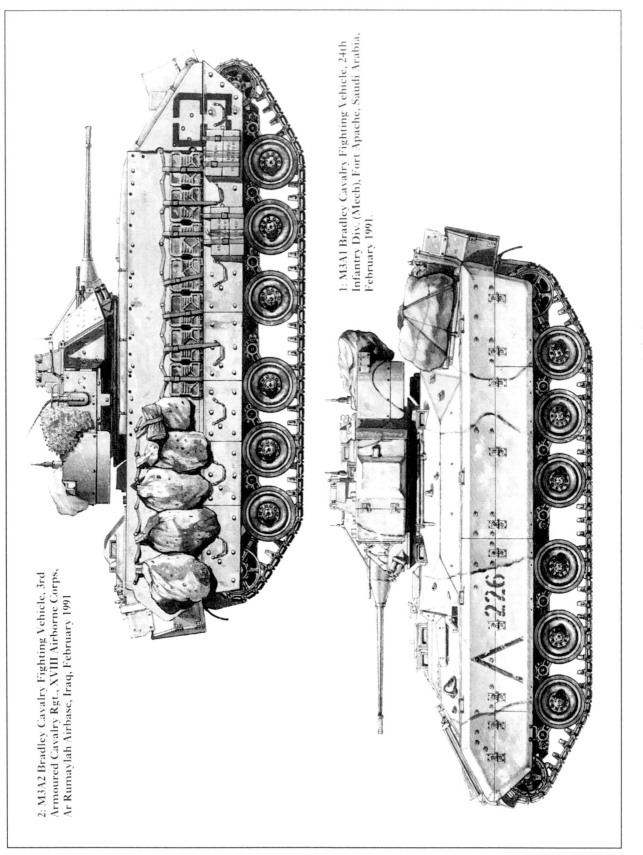

2: M3A2 Bradley Cavalry Fighting Vehicle, 3rd
Armoured Cavalry Rgt., XVIII Airborne Corps,
Ar Rumaylah Airbase, Iraq, February 1991

1: M3A1 Bradley Cavalry Fighting Vehicle, 24th
Infantry Div. (Mech), Fort Apache, Saudi Arabia,
February 1991.

A

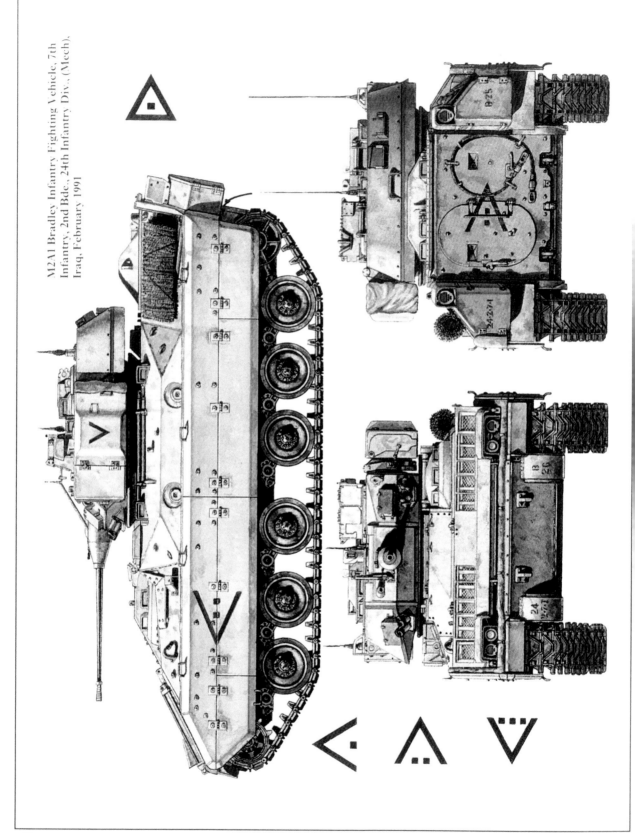

M2A1 Bradley Infantry Fighting Vehicle, 7th Infantry, 2nd Bde., 24th Infantry Div., (Mech). Iraq, February 1991

M3A1 Bradley Cavalry Fighting Vehicle, Task Force 1-8 Cavalry, 2nd 'Blackjack' Bde., 1st Cavalry Div., Iraq, February 1991

M2A2 BRADLEY IFV

3rd Armoured Cavalry Brigade, XVIII Airborne Corps, Iraq, February 1991

SPECIFICATIONS

Crew: 3+6 dismounts
Combat Weight: 66,000 lbs
Power-to-weight ratio: 18.2 hp/t
Hull length: 258 inches
Width: 129 inches (142 inches with reactive armour)
Height to turret roof: 117 inches
Engine: Cummins VTA-903T 14.8 litre 4 cycle, 600 hp diesel
Transmission: GE HMPT-500-3 hydromechanical transmission with hydrostatic steering and multi-disc, oil-cooled brakes
Fuel capacity: 175 gallons
Max. road speed: 38 mph
Max. cross-country speed: 30 mph
Max. range: 250 miles
Fuel consumption: 0.7 gallons per mile
Slope: 60% (40% side slope)
Obstacle: 36 inch wall, 100 inch trench
Main gun: M242 Bushmaster chain gun
Muzzle velocity: 4.660 ft/s (M919 APFSDS-T)
Effective range: + 1.25 miles
Stowed gun rounds: 300 ready, 600 stowed
Elevation: -10 to +60 degrees
Missile: BGM-71D TOW-2
Effective range: 12,300 ft.
Stowed missiles rounds: 2 ready, 5 stowed
Secondary armament: co-axial M240C 7.62mm light machine gun; two M231 5.56mm FPW

KEY

1. M2A2 applique steel armour
2. Armoured headlight cover
3. Folded fording screen
4. Driver's instrument panel
5. Driver's steering yoke
6. Driver's clutch
7. M242 Bushmaster 25mm gun
8. Smoke grenade dischargers
9. TOW "twin-pack" armoured launcher box (folded)
10. Articulation arm for commander's exterior bead sight
11. Armoured cover of Integrated Sight Unit (ISU)
12. Gunner's turret traverse handle
13. Breech of M242 25mm cannon
14. Vehicle commander's sight
15. Commander's control
16. Commander's periscope
17. Vehicle radio antenna
18. Instruction pamphlet stowage
19. Commander's turret hatch (open)
20. Rear turret stowage rack
21. Stowage rack for 7.62mm ammunition box
22. Commander's seat
23. Halon fire extinguisher
24. Armoured roof hatch for reloading TOW launcher
25. Dismount squad seat
26. Covered fording screen
27. 25mm ammunition box stowage
28. Armoured rear light
29. External stowage box
30. Rear exit ramp (closed)
31. Floor stowage bin cover
32. TOW missile stowage
33. Idler wheel
34. Gunner's seat
35. 25mm ammunition ready stowage
36. Turret basket
37. Engine firewall
38. Driver's seat
39. Driver's stowage
40. Drive sprocket

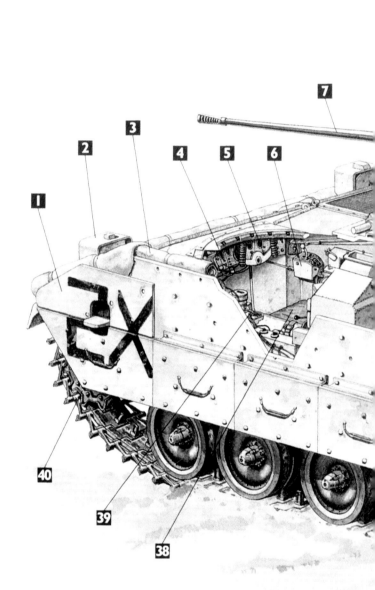

D

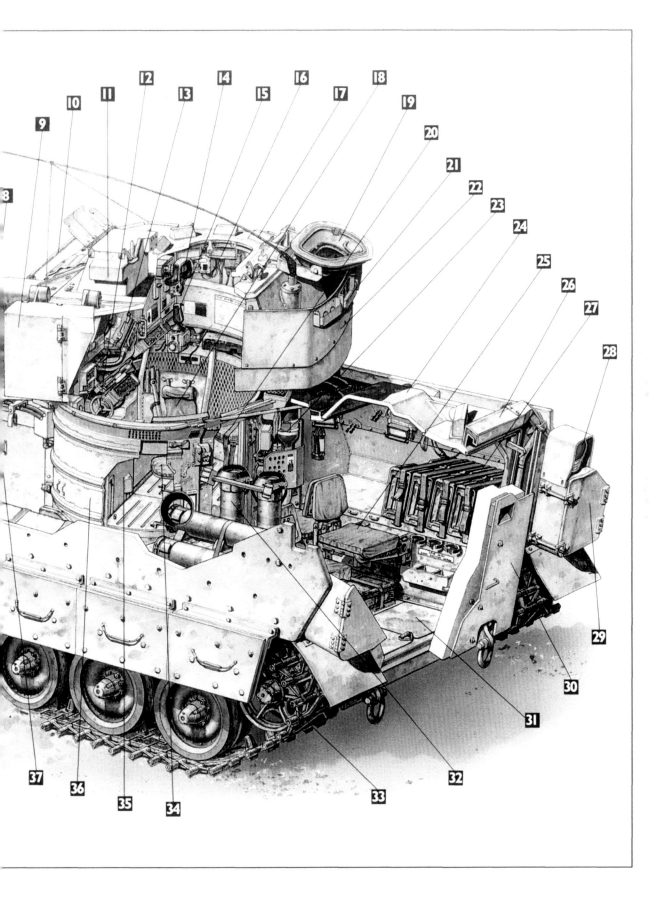

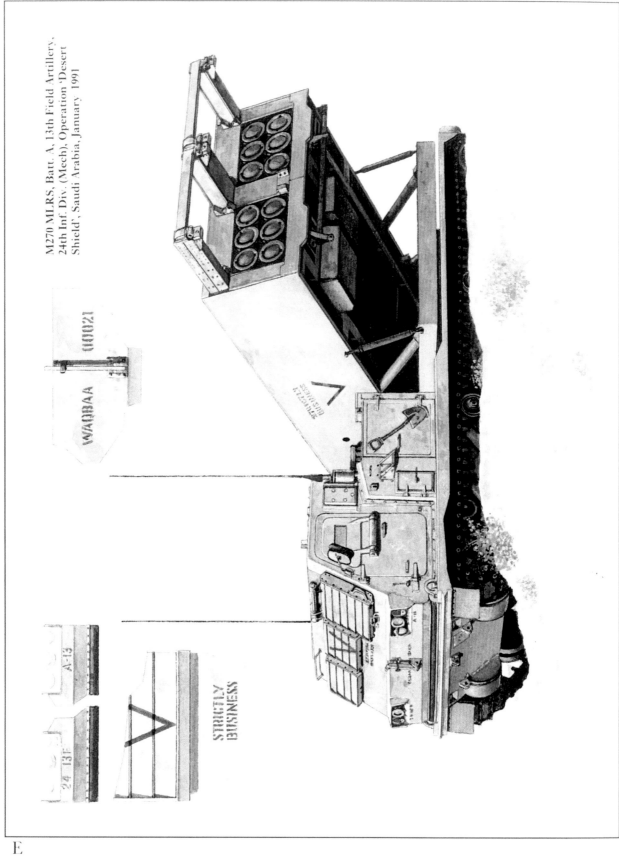

M270 MLRS, Batt. A, 13th Field Artillery, 24th Inf. Div. (Mech), Operation 'Desert Shield', Saudi Arabia, January 1991

E

1: M270 MLRS, Batt.C, 4th Bn., 27th Field Artillery (MLRS),
2nd Armoured Cavalry Regt., Saudi Arabia, February 1991

2: M270 MLRS, Batt.B, USArmy Field Artillery Regt.
(MLRS), Iraq, February 1991

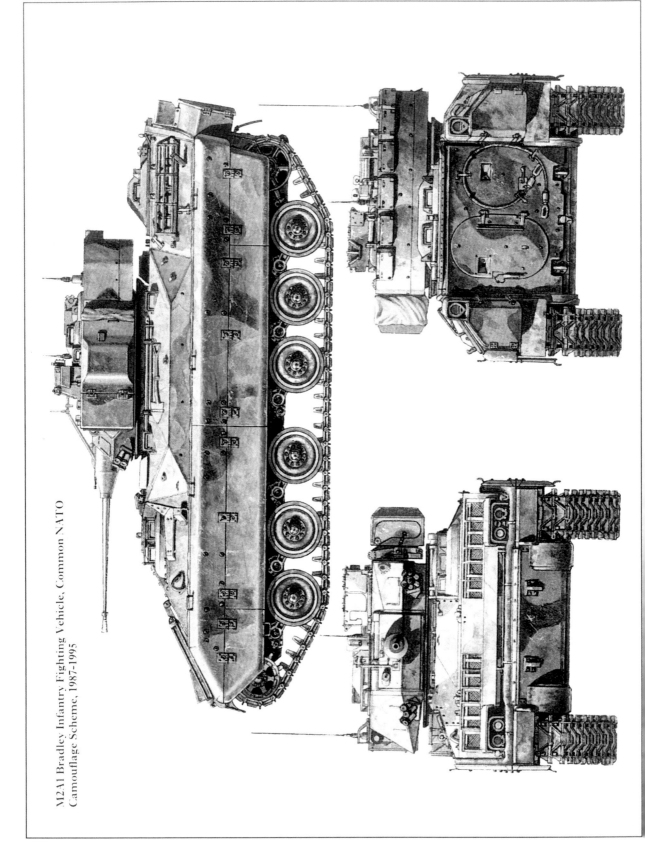

M2A1 Bradley Infantry Fighting Vehicle, Common NATO
Camouflage Scheme, 1987–1995

tion of ammunition stowage within the Bradley in the hope of reducing the probability of ammunition fires. The armour increased the weight of the Bradley by 20% (7.3 metric tons). Although the first 662 production Bradley A2s were powered by the same 500 hp Cummins diesel as earlier versions, starting in May 1989, the 600 hp VTA-903T turbo-charged diesel was introduced to restore the vehicle's mobility to that of the earlier Bradley A0 and A1 series. In 1990, the US Army began to fund a programme to upgrade all of the 1,371 Bradley A1s to A2 standards at the Red River Army Depot. Upgrades of the Bradley A0 variants to the A2 standards were not undertaken due to the higher costs that these upgrades require. The final production funding for the Bradley was contained in the Fiscal Year 1994 budget, and the final production vehicle for the US Army was manufactured in 1995. Production of the Bradley is expected to continue for several years due to exports. The first major customer was the Royal Saudi Arabian Army, which expects to receive the first of its 400 Bradleys in 1998.

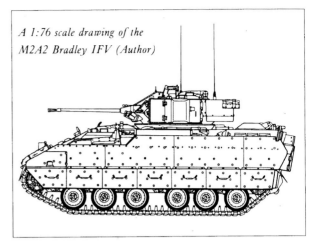

A 1:76 scale drawing of the M2A2 Bradley IFV (Author)

called 'plain vanilla Bradleys': that is M2A0 and M2A1). At the time of the fighting, only one division, the 1st Infantry Div., was still equipped with a large number of M2A0s (but its cavalry unit, 1-4 Cavalry, had M3A2s); two more had the M2A1 (24th Infantry and 3rd Armored Divisions), while

PERFORMANCE IN 'DESERT STORM'

The Bradley played an integral role in operations by the US Army during Operation 'Desert Storm'. About 2,200 Bradleys were deployed in Saudi Arabia in February 1991 when the ground campaign began; the relative breakdown was 19% A0, 33% A1 and 48% A2. Not all these vehicles saw combat; many of the older A0s were left in theatre as attrition spares. No programme was undertaken to up-armour Bradleys in the field as was the case with M1A1 Abrams tanks. Unlike the M1A1 upgrade, the Bradley A2 armour package could not be installed in field depots but required factory rebuilding, making any such uparmouring impractical. Instead, 692 Bradley A2s were shipped from POMCUS storage in Europe or straight off the assembly line from FMC Corp in San Jose. They were used to replace older production Bradleys (sometimes

The Bradley allows the infantry to fight dismounted when terrain does not favour mechanised action. Here, a squad from the 15th Infantry, 24th Infantry Division (Mech) carry out at dismount exercise at Ft. Stewart, Georgia while the M2A2 IFV provides fire support. (Author)

From the outset, the Bradley A2 was designed to accept reactive armour tiles for additional protection against shaped charge warheads such as those found on anti-tank rockets and missiles. Two competitive designs were developed, and in 1993, the Martin Marietta/Rafael design was selected. In the field configuration, the tiles are contained in steel boxes, which are covered with a camouflaged fabric cover. (United Defense LP)

two other divisions had mostly been equipped with M2A2s (1st Cavalry and 1st Armored Divisions). Both the 2nd Armored Cavalry and 3rd Armored Cavalry Brigades were mostly equipped with M2A2 and M3A2 Bradleys.

The armoured cavalry regiments were truly formidable, with a total of 116 M1A1 Abrams tanks and 132 Bradleys. Each regiment had three squadrons each with three troops. An armoured cavalry troop had nine tanks and 12 Bradley CFVs, for a total of 41 tanks and 38 Bradley CFVs per squadron.

One of the few major shortages at the beginning of the fighting concerned 25 mm ammunition. Eventually, about three million rounds were shipped to Saudi Arabia but there was still a shortage of the new M919 depleted uranium penetrator projectile for attacking armoured targets. The M919 penetrator had only entered low-rate initial production in 1990, but when war broke out, the programme was accelerated. In some units, the gunners were instructed to conserve these rounds by first firing a ranging round, followed by no more than three rounds for killing effect. A 1st Armoured Div. company commander later noted with satisfaction that even in the confusion of night fighting, there was the eerie monotony of Bradleys firing with a distinctive

'crack...pause...crack-crack-crack'. In the event, the ammunition shortage did not prove a problem as the Bradley gunners averaged only six rounds for each enemy armoured vehicle destroyed, a tribute to excellent gunnery training.

Few of the infantry or armoured divisions fought with peacetime battalion organisation during 'Desert Storm'. In most cases, the companies of mechanised infantry and tank battalions were cross-attached to form task force organisations for better integrated combined-arms battle tactics. For example, Task Force 3-15th Infantry (24th Infantry Division) consisted of two of the battalion's usual Bradley companies teamed with two M1A1 Abrams tank companies from 1-64th Armor; the remaining two Bradley companies were in turn cross-attached to Task Force 1-64th Armor. Tactics depended on terrain. The tanks often took the lead due to their superior armour, with Bradley companies often forming a protective screen on the flanks. However, once Iraqi defences were reached, the Bradley companies moved forward to add their firepower to the fray.

Successes in Combat

The combat performance of the Bradley in 'Desert Storm' was widely praised. One of its most appricated features was its high speed,

The M2A2 and M3A2 had entered production only two years before 'Desert Storm', and many US Army units were still equipped with older vehicles. As a result, over 600 new Bradley A2s were rushed to the Gulf to re-equip as many units as possible before the ground campaign began. As is usual with infantry vehicles, the Bradleys soon began to resemble gypsy caravans with a plethora of tents and personal gear festooned on the outside of the vehicle. During the fighting, many vehicles also had additional 25 mm ammunition containers lashed to the side armour. (United Defense LP)

A M2A2 IFV of C Company, 1-5th Cavalry, 1st Cavalry Division under the protection of a camouflage net in Saudi Arabia shortly before the outbreak of the ground campaign against the Iraqi army in February 1991. (United Defense LP)

This rare shot shows one of a handful of Bradleys fitted with the VLQ-7 Stingray electro-optical jammer deployed to Saudi Arabia for 'Desert Storm'. This medium energy laser device was designed to blind electro-optical sensors such as tank sights, and was fielded as a possible response to Iraqi use of lasers to blind troops.

factor in vehicle survivability since it made the vehicle very difficult for Iraqi RPG gunners or other anti-tank weapons to accurately target when on the move. The Bradley's thermal imaging night sight proved efficacious in adverse weather conditions such as sand storms, giving it the ability to fight when Iraqi armoured vehicles were blind. Many crewmen regarded the Bradley's thermal imaging sight as superior to that of the M1A1 Abrams, and noted that they could identify targets at longer ranges than the tanks. Although there had been concerns before the war over the vehicle's transmission, during the fighting there were no reports of transmission failures. Bradley operational readiness rates were 90 per cent or higher both before and during combat operations. Some Bradley commanders suggested that the transmission be modified with a faster reverse gear to enable the Bradley to keep pace with the Abrams in all-azimuth firefights.

enabling it to keep pace with the charging M1A1 Abrams tanks. This was no small consideration, as the slower M113-derived vehicles caused considerable problems in many units due to their slow speed in the sand. Many Bradley commanders considered the high vehicle speed to be a major

The firepower of the Bradley proved to be hugely impressive. Official US Army sources reported that the 25 mm Bushmaster cannon was 'lethal beyond all expectations'. Although most Bradley gunners had been taught to use the TOW

M3A1 CFVs of the 1-4th Cav., 24th Inf. Div.(Mech) in Saudi Arabia before the outbreak of the ground campaign against Iraq, the vertical rear stowage bins are a characteristic feature of this version; the first 284 Bradley A1s still had the angled rear turret bins. This unit was one of a few US Army units to pattern paint camouflage during 'Desert Storm'; the other battalions of the division all used the normal overall CARC tan scheme. (Frank DeSisto-Intrepid Museum)

An M2A1 IFV moves past the wreck of an Iraqi BMP-1 during the short ground campaign of 'Desert Storm'. The US Army was very satisfied with the combat performance of the Bradley in the war. The Soviet BMP-1 was more sternly judged by its adversary, due to its propensity of suffer ammunition fires which often led to a major internal explosion, blowing its turret off as is seen in this case. (United Defense LP)

to engage enemy tanks, crews soon learned that older types such as the Chinese Type 59 could be knocked out with 25 mm fire, especially when using depleted uranium rounds from the sides.

Some idea of the capabilities of the Bradley can be garnered from an actual engagement. Around 1100 on G-Day+3, Task Force 4-7th Infantry of the 1st Armoured Division reached an Iraqi defensive position on 'Medina Ridge' held by mixed elements of the Republican Guard's Medina Division. The M2A2 Bradley of the company master gunner, Staff Sgt. Charles Peters, spotted several Iraqi vehicles on a slope below his position. Peters destroyed one BMP with three rounds of 25 mm AP ammunition then switched to HE to rake the Iraqi infantry fleeing into nearby trenches. Peters switched back to AP and destroyed another BMP which exploded in a fireball as its ammunition ignited. Peters engaged a third vehicle which did not explode. As the dust cleared, the reason became frighteningly apparent: it was a T-72M tank and it began to fire on the Bradley company. Peters quickly engaged the TOW twin pack, but it seemed an eternity before it rose into firing position. Fortunately, the Iraqi gunnery was poor, and Peters launched a TOW-2 missile which destroyed the T-72M in another

fireball. Peters switched back to the 25 mm and destroyed a third BMP. The engagement had taken little more than a minute.

The 25 mm gun was the primary weapon used by the Bradley, being used especially to engage Iraqi infantry and light armoured vehicles. For example, in the 3rd Armored Division, 10,214 rounds of 25mm ammunition were expended during the war, compared to only 101 TOW missiles. The one unpopular weapon on the Bradley was the 7.62 mm co-axial machine gun, which jammed repeatedly. The TOW missile was well regarded, although there were some problems with the reliability of the TOW twin-pack launcher; many gunners were also unhappy with the slow speed in elevating the launcher. The main problem with TOW was the lack of a laser rangefinder in the Bradley's fire control system. As a result, it was often difficult for the gunners to determine whether the Iraqi target was within range. In spite of these problems, the TOW missile was highly regarded, and gave the Bradley a vital degree of anti-tank capability.

Before the war broke out, the US Army learned that the Iraqi Army was deploying electro-optical dazzlers on some of their best tanks such as the T-72M. The dazzler is a modulated infrared device that counteracts wire-guided anti-tank missiles such as the TOW. The TOW guidance functions by the use of an optical tracker in the missile launch system that monitors a small flare or lamp in the tail of the missile. The dazzler operates at the same wavelength as the flare, and as the missile approaches its intended target, the dazzler confuses the missile tracker as to which is the real missile signal. Steps were introduced to develop counter-measures to the dazzler, but the Iraqis do not seem to have made very effective use of these systems. There were only two probable cases where the TOW was decoyed by dazzlers, and in one of these cases the interference caused the missile to veer into a neighboring tank, destroying it instead of the intended target. The US Army developed its own dazzlers, the AN/VLQ-6 Hardhat and AN/VLQ-8, but it would appear that none reached service before the end of the war.

Another concern of the US Army regarding Iraqi secret weapons was the possibility of Iraqi use of laser blinding weapons. There had been reports from the time of the Iran-Iraq war of 1980-88 that the Iraqis had occasionally used lasers to blind advancing Iranian infantry. It as not clear if this was deliberate, or simply due to inadvertent damage caused by laser rangefinders or laser designators. In the event, the US Army decided to ship two of its experimental Bradley Stingray vehicles to Saudi Arabia. Although the vehicles were deployed, no authorisation was given for the use of their laser systems.

The protective systems of the Bradley were favourably received. Contrary to pre-war critcism that the Bradley's aluminium armour would burn when struck by tank rounds, no such events occured. The compartmentation on the Bradley and the new DuPont Kevlar spall liners on the Bradley A2 reduced casualties when the vehicle was hit, and the automatic fire extinguishing system was found to be effective. Sadly, most of the damage suffered by Bradleys was due to 'own goals'. According to official US Army sources, only three Bradleys were lost to hostile fire while 17 were lost to friendly fire, mainly M1A1 tank guns. For example on 27 February 1991 during the 'Battle of Norfolk' by the 2nd Armoured Division, US units became intermixed with Iraqi units due to the poor visibility and chaotic battle conditions. In the confusion, three Bradleys of Bravo Company, 1-41st Infantry were hit by M1A1 120 mm tank rounds, destroying all three vehicles, killing four soldiers and wounding 18. The official US Department of Defense report on the war concluded that '... the Bradley A2 model's survivability improvements proved effective as evidenced by several examples of vehicles which took significant hits without flash fires or catastrophic loss. Most damage was found to be penetrator related with little damage from spall. Unless combustibles or ammunition were in the penetrator path, there was little collateral damage. Fire supression systems worked extremely well...' However, the fact that fire from friendly forces caused more Bradley losses than enemy fire confirms the need for a combat vehicle identification system to prevent fratricide.'

The Bradleys fared much better than the 'Bimps', the Soviet BMPs used by the Iraqi Republican Guard. Like the Soviet tanks, the BMPs had a tendency to suffer catastrophic internal ammunition fires when hit, the resultant explosion often gutting the vehicle and blowing off its turret. This was chiefly the result of the concentration of the turret ammunition, the lack of compartmentation of the ammunition or other protective features.

Scout units were not entirely happy with the Bradley due to its height and large size. Before the war broke out, some units began experimenting with the use of HMMWV light trucks for the scout platoons. However, this was not an ideal solution, as commanders found that they often had to recall HMMWV scout units due to their vulnerability to artillery fire.

Ideally, a smaller armoured vehicle was desired and the cancelled M800 ARSV probably would have satisfied this requirement. Currently, the US Army is intending to replace the Bradley in the scouting role with the FSV (Future Scout Vehicle) early in the next century.

The employment of Bradleys in 'Desert Storm' contained several surprises. In many of the engagements, the infantry never dismounted for combat. This was due to the unusually fast pace of the action, and the open desert terrain that favoured mounted action. Mechanised infantry tactics in desert conditions straddle classic conceptions of infantry and cavalry. The armament of the Bradley proved to be a good balance with that on the supporting tanks. The decision to equip the Bradley with an anti-tank missile was validated, as Bradleys often encountered tanks and were able to deal with them without requiring the support of tanks. Indeed, the battles against the Iraqi Army accentuated the virtues of heavy mechanised infantry. It would be imprudent to draw too broad a lesson from this war. In other environments and against other enemies, mechanised infantry may have to adopt rather different tactics. But 'Desert Storm' did highlight the trends since the last century which have seen an incredible increase in infantry firepower, protection and mobility in high intensity conflicts.

Recent Upgrade Programmes

In the wake of 'Desert Storm', work began on a series of improvements based on lessons learned in the fighting. This Phase I upgrade will probably include the incorporation of a GPS terminal and compass to assist in vehicle navigation, the addition of a laser rangefinder to the fire control system, the addition of the AN/VAS-3 Driver's Thermal Viewer (DTV), a simple IFF capability, a AN/VLQ-6 or VLQ-8 missile countermeasure device and internal stowage improvements. These upgrades were planned for 1,433 vehicles including 131 A0s, 239 A1s and 933 A2s. The resulting

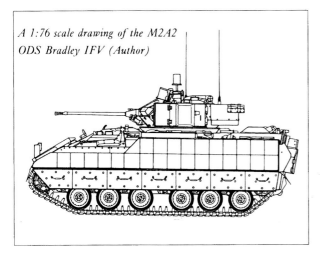

A 1:76 scale drawing of the M2A2 ODS Bradley IFV (Author)

version has been tenatively called the Bradley A2ODS (Operation Desert Storm). The drawing here shows a M2A2ODS with the missile countermeasure device mounted above the gunner's sight, and the reactive armour package.

As a longer term effort, the US Army would like to initiate a Phase 2 upgrade to incorporate the digital data handling system (IVIS inter-vehicular information system) from the M1A2 Abrams tank into the Bradley, as well as the Vehicle Integrated Defense System, a new package of defensive systems to defeat anti-tank missiles and other threats. This version, the Bradley A3, will include a databus core electronics upgrade, digital information displays, command and control software upgrades, and full digital integration of all ODS improvements. This will also be the first version of the Bradley with the Texas Instruments IBAS (Improved Bradley Acquisition System) which includes second generation focal plane array thermal sights for both the commander and gunner, and a completely redesigned FCS which includes an autotracking system. The Bradley A3 development programme started in 1994 and modification of Bradley A2s into A3s is expected to begin in the late 1990s and extend to 2010, with about 1,600 vehicles eventually upgraded.

VARIANTS

COMVAT

The COMVAT (Combat Vehicle Armament Technology, originally CVAST: Combat Vehicle Armaments Technology) was developed in the early 1980s as a potential response to the advent of the BMP-2 and a follow-on to the BMP. COMVAT originally consisted of a new turret and armament package developed by FMC and Ares Inc. based around a 35 mm gun; McDonnell Douglas also offered a 30 mm version of th existing M242, called the Bushmaster 2 or the 30 mm ASP. A new gun system is being developed now by Alliant Techsystems with cased telescoped ammunition. This programme aims to increase the effective range and penetration power of the

The CVAST was one of the early attempts to up-arm the Bradley to respond to future Soviet infantry vehicle developments. In the event, the new BMP-3 is not well armoured, and the end of the Cold War has pushed the follow-on COMVAT programme into a low-priority slot. (United Defense LP)

ADATS

Following the cancellation of the US Army M247 Sgt. York DIVAD, in 1988 the US Army selected the Martin Marietta/Oerlikon MIM-146 ADATS missile system as its new air defence system to operate in the forward area of heavy divisions to defend against enemy aircraft and helicopters. The Canadian Army had already ordered this system and mounted it on modified M113 chassis; the US Army selected the Bradley chassis instead with plans to build 562 ADATS vehicles. Initial operational testing and evaluation trials that ran through May 1990 found reliability, availability, and maintainability problems with the missile system. The Congress deleted the initial procurement funding from the 1991 budget, and in 1992, citing the reduced threat from the former Soviet Union, the Pentagon terminated the programme.

weapon, which has been designed to be easily scaled up from 30 mm to 45 mm. There has been little effort made to actually begin retrofitting the Bradley with such a weapon, as the BMP-3 is not sufficiently well armoured to resist the existing 25 mm gun. However, the US Army has continued to examine larger calibre guns for the Bradley as a fall-back should new threats appear.

Bradley Stinger Fighting Vehicle

In 1992, following the retirement of the M163 Vulcan air defense system and the cancellation of the MIM-146 ADATS programme, the US Army decided to adapt the M2A2 Bradley so as to provide additional air defence for mechanised units. In the initial stage, 267 vehicles were modified by

The Bradley was selected as the chassis for the ill-fated MIM-146 ADATS air defense missile system, which was eventually cancelled due to the low priority afforded tactical air defense within the US Army. The system was first deployed in the Canadian Army, but uses a M113 chassis. (Martin Marietta)

The poor automotive performance of the M981 FIST artillery forward observer vehicle in 'Desert Storm' has led to plans to fit the laser designator and other specialised equipment on a modified Bradley, called the Bradley FIST. The designator is fitted in the armoured box in place of the usual TOW missile launcher. It is not clear if the US Army will be able to afford these new vehicles. (United Defense LP)

internal stowage changes which permitted carrying a five-man Stinger squad and six Stinger missiles. The two Stinger teams dismount to use their weapons and the Bradley is simply a means to transport the squad. This was a less than satisfactory solution to the problem, and in 1993, the Army announced plans to field the Enhanced Bradley Stinger Fighting Vehicle (BSFV-E). Unlike the BSFV, the enhanced BSFV test-bed mounted Stinger launchers in the turret in place of the usual TOW launchers; the vehicles will be converted from Bradley A2ODS vehicles. Several competitive designs were considered, and the development award went to Boeing in April 1995. Boeing will produce eight BSFV-E vehicles for trials and may manufacture about 60 additional production kits after October 1998 when the tests are completed.

Bradley FIST

During 'Desert Storm' in 1991, the US Army artillery found that its forward observer vehicle, the M981 FIST (Fire Support Team) based on the M113 APC chassis was too slow to keep up with newer vehicles. The 1st Cavalry Division actually took some of the equipment from the FIST-V and mounted it on Bradleys, which they called Bradley FS (Fire Support). As a result of these experiences, a programme was initiated to transfer the specialised FIST equipment including the Ground Vehicle Laser-Locator Designator, into the Bradley. The laser designator will be mounted in a new armoured container in place of the usual TOW launcher. The Army would like to acquire an initial batch of 185 FIST vehicles, though as many as 560 has been considered.

Stingray

In September 1982, the US Army awarded Martin Marietta a development contract for the AN/VLQ-7 Stingray electro-optical countermeasures system. The programme was aimed at developing a vehicle-mounted, medium-energy laser weapon capable of crazing the optics and vision ports on opposing tactical vehicles, the destruction of electro-optical sensors, and the opaqueing of helicopter or jet aircraft canopies. The system was mounted on a Bradley turret for testing purposes. The Stingray works by emitting a low energy laser beam which is scanned over the battlefield. On striking an optical surface such as a tank sight, the laser light is reflected back, allowing the Stingray sensor to determine its location. The Stingray is then switched to jamming mode, and uses a medium energy laser beam to attack the enemy sensors it has located. The Stingray has remained a controversial concept, as their is general public revulsion at the idea of a weapon that

One of the most exotic versions of the Bradley is the Stingray, fitted with the VLQ-7 laser electro-optical jammer. This system scans the battlefield with a low energy laser which detects enemy sensors, and then attacks them with an intense beam of medium energy laser light, jamming their circuits or damaging their optics. Stingray could be used to blind enemy troops and the public outcry which ensued has put a damper on such programmes.

As a stop-gap to replace the ADATS, some Bradleys were adapted to carry Stinger missile teams into combat. As a longer-term solution, the US Army is working on an enhanced Bradley Stinger Fighting Vehicle which will have the Stingers fitted in an armoured box launcher. This is the initial prototype of the system developed by FMC Corp, which places four Stinger launchers in a large armoured box in place of the usual TOW anti-tank missiles. (Author)

A heavily modified Bradley chassis was used as the basis for the LOSAT, a tank destroyer armed with hyper-velocity kinetic energy missiles on a retractable launcher in the centre of the vehicle. With the end of the Cold War, the need for such a vehicle has diminished, and the programme has been put into limbo as a technology demonstrator. (United Technologies LP)

could be used to blind enemy troops. Two Bradley Stingrays were deployed during Operation 'Desert Storm', but did not actually use the Stingray system. There is a lightweight version, called Outrider, mounted on HMMWV light trucks for Marine Corps' operations.

LOSAT

LOSAT (Line-Of-Sight-Anti-Tank) is a hypervelocity laser-guided anti-tank missile system mounted on a modified Bradley hull. It was developed by the US Army to replace the M901 Improved-TOW Vehicle (ITV). With the end of the Cold War, the Army recommended terminating the LOSAT programme as a cost cutting measure in October 1993.

However, the Army is still funding the programme at a low level to keep the technology alive, but may use the M8 AGS chassis instead of the Bradley should the programme proceed.

ETAS

The Elevated Target Acquisition System was an attempt to develop a sensor pod, mounted on the end of a telescoping pole assembly. The rationale behind this is that by fitting such a sensor to the M3 CFV scout vehicle, the M3 could hide behind terrain, protecting itself from counterfire, while the sensor package is elevated high above for a

better view of the surroundings. Such a pod would probably includes a thermal viewer, a low-probability-of-intercept radar, a laser rangefinder and a radio frequency interferometer. At the moment, the programme is in limbo.

M987 FVS

The basic Bradley chassis also forms the basis for the M987 Fighting Vehicle System armoured transporter. This is currently used as the basis of the M270 MLRS multiple rocket launcher vehicle. A number of other derivatives have also been examined, including the XM1007 AFARV tank re-ammunition vehicle, the Firefinder mobile radar vehicle using a Hughes phased-array surveillance radar, the XM1070 Electronic Fighting Vehicle System, and the XM4 Command and Control Vehicle (C2V). A total of of 58 of the M1070 EFVS are expected to be ordered by the US Army as part of the XM5 Ground-Based Common Sensor-Heavy for use in the electronic warfare mission, and orders for the M4 C2V vehicle are also expected.

M270 MLRS

The M270 Multiple Launch Rocket System entered development early 1976 as a means to supplement more conventional towed and self-propelled artillery. In May 1980, the US Army selected LTV as the prime contractor for MLRS.

The MLRS uses the M993 chassis, a derivative of the M987 FVS chassis. Production began in 1982, the first low-rate production launchers were delivered to the Field Artillery School at Ft. Sill in February 1982, the first production rockets in May 1982, and the first production launchers in August 1982. MLRS was fielded for the first time in early 1983 with field artillery battalions of the 1st Infantry Division (Mechanised) in Ft. Riley, KS. The US Army has acquired 725 MLRS launchers and the Marine Corps has ordered a further 18; total Army orders for the MLRS rocket have totalled over 555,000.

The MLRS idea proved so attractive that a European consortium was formed to licence produce it; the first batch were completed in 1989, final deliveries being completed in 1993. The European NATO countries planned to acquire 350 SPLL launch vehicles and 190,000 rockets, but only 284 MLRS launchers were built: Germany (150); France (55); UK (57); Italy (22). France began fielding the second of two 24-SPLL regiments by the end of 1995; Germany completed fielding 72 systems in eight battalions in 1994. Italy deployed 20 systems by the end of 1994. Other customers for MLRS have included the Netherlands (22 launchers ordered in 1988); Bahrain (nine launchers delivered in 1992); Japan (36 launchers with partial co-assembly in by Nissan and delivery by 1996); Israel (nine launch-

Besides the normal rockets, the MLRS can also carry and fire two of the larger MGM-140 ATACMS missiles, used for deep attack of key enemy positions. The current versions of the missile drop a payload of submunition grenades on the target, but future versions will use the BAT guided submunition. (US Army)

gramme in favour of pursuing its own BAT munition, but France is still developing the smart weapon at a slow pace. The US Army has been developing the M836 SADARM (Sense and Destroy Armor) munition for the MLRS which dispenses six smart submunitions for counter-battery or anti-armour missions. This programme was put on hold in 1995 and will probably be replaced by the MLRS Smart Tactical Rocket (MSTAR). Two other new guided rocket programmes are the MITS and Multi-Pltform Launcher. MITS (Multiple Independently Targetable Submunitions) is being developed by Lockheed and mates a GPS and inertial guidance package to an MLRS rocket with a penetrator warhead for attacking bunkers and other targets. The Multi-Platform Launcher is an effort to field a low-cost inertial system for the MLRS rocket.

The MLRS launcher is also capable of firing the MGM-140 ATACMS (Army Tactical Missile System), a deep attack, semi-ballistic missile. Two ATACMS missiles are carried per launcher and the initial Block 1 version uses an APAM submunition warhead much like the normal MLRS rocket but with 950 dual purpose M74 bomblets. The Army is currently embarking on development of the Block 1A extended range version of ATACMS, substituting more fuel for fewer submunitions. The Block 2 (also called BAT Carrier) will employ a BAT anti-armour precision guided munition. A third derivative, called Block 2A ER BAT Carrier, will carry the Improved BAT (IBAT) to extended ranges.

The MLRS was first used in combat by US Army units during Operation 'Desert Storm' in 1991. A total of 189 MLRS launchers were deployed to the Gulf equipping seven battalions. In addition, the British Army deployed a single battery with 12 launchers with the 1st Armoured Division. A total of 9,660 MLRS rockets were fired during the war. The system was considered to be extremely effective, and one of the few complaints (by the Marine Corps) is that there were not enough of them for all the fire missions required. Iraqi troops called the incoming munitions 'steel rain'. Two MLRS batteries (18 launchers), were specifically earmarked for conducting deep-strike missions with ATACMS. The first

ers ordered in 1993); and Greece (nine launchers to be delivered by 1996). Both Turkey and Saudi Arabia ordered MLRS systems but had to back off before delivery due to funding problems.

The basic M26 MLRS rocket has a warhead containing 644 M77 anti-materiel/anti-personnel munitions which are dispensed in midair and cover an area of about 200 feet in diameter. Each MLRS launcher can deliver 7,728 M77 grenades in less than one minute. Germany developed a scatterable mine for the MLRS Phase 2, called the AT-2, but it has been the only country to acquire this type. The Phase 3 MLRS was a multinational effort to develop the Terminally Giuided Warhead (TGW), for attacking massed Soviet tank formations. The US dropped out of the promission was conducted by Alpha Battery, 6/27th Field Artillery on 18 January 1991 destroying an Iraqi SA-2 'Guideline' air defence missile battery. ATACMS were used to attack Iraqi radars, and during an attack on a bridge, ATACMS succeeded in destroying about 200 trucks and other vehicles. A grand total of 32 missiles were expended during 24 fire missions out of the theatre inventory of 105 missiles.

THE PLATES

Bradley Camouflage and Markings

Starting in 1973, the US Army combat vehicles began to be painted in a new four colour camouflage scheme developed by the US Army Mobility Equipment Research and Development Command (MERDC) at Ft. Belvoir. Some early production Bradleys were painted in in the MERDC patterns, mainly in the Winter Verdant scheme. However, this scheme never became common. In the early 1980s, the Army decided to adopt the new CARC (chemical agent resistent coating) paint which was specifically formulated to permit troops to uses chemical decontamination solutions on the vehicle. There had been a problem with the earlier paints used with the MERDC camouflage which tended to peel off when subjected to strong decontamination solutions. As a result, for several years in the mid-1980s, new Bradleys tended to appear in a monotone finish of overall FS 34079 Forest Green in CARC paint without the MERDC camouflage. The reason for this was that at the same time, discussions were taking place in NATO to adopt a common camouflage pattern so as to avoid the problem of each army's vehicles being easily distinguished by Warsaw Pact intelligence by their different colours. In the mid-1980s, NATO agreed to accept a German-designed system using three colours: green, black and brown.

This system did not become common in the US Army until 1987 and the colours employed are FS 30051 Green, FS 34094 Brown and FS 37030 Black. Details of typical Bradley markings in the early 1980s can be found in the previous Osprey publication, Vanguard Number 43.

When first shipped to Saudi Arabia, many Bradleys were finished overall Forest Green or in the common NATO pattern camouflage. To better blend in to the local desert, US vehicles were repainted in FS 33446 Tan, also known as CARC Tan 686.

Like the paints for the new NATO scheme, this is a special permanent paint which does not dissolve when subjected to cleaning by common chemical warfare decontamination solutions.

Basic markings during 'Desert Storm' followed usual US Army practices. Before the ground campaign, most vehicles had 'bumper codes' on the front and rear which give basic unit data on the left and company/vehicle number on the right. The numbering pattern for line combat vehicles is generally: 66 (battalion commander), 65 (battalion executive officer); 11, 12, etc. (lst Platoon), 21, 22, etc. (2nd Platoon), 31, 32, etc. (3rd Platoon). These bumper codes were overpainted before the fighting began in some units. Many US Army units also adopted special tactical markings, sometimes called the 'Spinning Vee', which was obviously inspired by Israeli Army markings. The chevrons rotate sequentially in a clock-wise direction: A Company (up); B Company (facing right); C Company (down); D Company (facing left). In some cases, all four Vees were combined in a diamond shape, probably indicating headquarters tanks. This system was adopted by most mechanised units of US Army VII 'Jayhawks' Corps. In the VII Corps, the chevron could have a two digit number added inside the chevron. This appears to have been a battalion code-number (first digit) followed by a platoon number. However, there were many exceptions as noted below. Shortly before G-Day, all combat vehicles had a large black upward chevron painted on the side as the accepted recognition marking for the Allied forces. In addition, a VS-17 identification panel was tied to the rear roof turret bustle rack of the Bradley. This is a 70 x 30 in. plastic sheet, fluorescent orange/red on one side and white on the reverse with green canvas reinforcement and tie-downs along the edges. It has been the standard method of aircraft recognition in the US Army since World War 2, and alternate colours include fluorescent yellow and blue.

Since 'Desert Storm', most US Army units have reverted back to the common NATO camouflage scheme. However, there are some exceptions, such as the 24th Infantry Division (Mechanised) at Ft. Stewart, GA and other rapid reaction units earmarked for potential deployment to the Middle East, which have retained their CARC Tan camouflage schemes.

Plate A1: *M3A1 Bradley Cavalry Fighting Vehicle, Task Force 2-4 Cavalry, 24th Infantry Division (Mechanized), Fort Apache, Saudi Arabia, February 1991*

'First in-Last Out'; the motto of the 4th Cavalry is evocative of their scouting mission, spearheading the way for the other combat elements of the 24th Infantry Div. during 'Desert Storm'. Unique to the Division, the 2nd Squadron used a simple camouflage pattern instead of the monotone CARC Tan found on most other vehicles. The basic faded Forest Green colour in which the vehicle arrived was partly retained, with swatches of the new CARC Tan painted over it. The colours were demarkated with thin bands about 1.5 in. wide of black paint. Before the start of 'Desert Storm', the Bradleys were painted with the familiar upward pointing chevron. The only other marking was a three digit tactical number, the M113s and M577s of the unit headquarters usually starting in a '0' (eg. 030, 090), while the 2nd Squadron Bradleys using numbers starting in '2' (eg. 213, 221, 226); the last two digits were probably issued sequentially.

Plate A2: *M3A2 Bradley Cavalry Fighting Vehicle, E Troop, 2nd Squadron, 3rd Armored Cavalry Regiment, XVIII Airborne Corps, Ar Rumaylah Airbase, Iraq, February 1991*

Typical of most BFVs during Operation Desert Storm, this M3A2 is finished in the overall CARC Tan. The 3rd ACR preferred to use troop letters rather than the 'Spinning-Vee' unit insignia used by many other US Army units during 'Desert Storm'. This consisted of the Troop letter followed by the Platoon number, in this scene E3 indicating the 3rd Platoon of E troop. The allied identification chevron was usually painted on the turret side since the hull chevron, usually on the

rear side, tended to become obscured by all the gear strung off the vehicle.

Plate B: *M2A1 Bradley Infantry Fighting Vehicle, 7th Infantry, 2nd Brigade, 24th Infantry Division (Mechanized), Iraq, February 1991*

This illustration shows the typical markings for Bradley IFVs during Desert Storm in the 24th 'Victory' Division. Like many US Army units, the division used a 'Spinning-Vee' system of markings, with the chevron representing the company, and the pips inside it indicating the platoon. So this vehicle is of 2nd Platoon, B Company. The style of the pips varied, some units like this one placing them in a horizontal row, other units plaing them in a vertical row as shown in the accompanying insert illustration. The V marking on the turret is the divisional insignia, which symbolised the divisional name.

Plate C: *M3A1 Bradley Cavalry Fighting Vehicle, Task Force 1-8 Cavalry, 2nd 'Blackjack' Brigade, 1st Cavalry Division, Iraq, February 1991*

This Bradley served with the scout platoon of the 1st Squadron, 8th Cavalry. This division followed the usual practice of the 'Spinning-Vee' insignia, but in this case, the scout platoon uses an '0' rather than a tactical number. The 1st Cavalry Division did not paint its bumper codes on the transmission housing as was the case with most units, but along the lower lip of the swimming deflector plate. In this case, the codes are obscured by a load of MREs (Meals Ready to Eat, or 'Meals Refused by Ethiopians' in troop slang). In this case, the bumber codes would read 1 CAV 1-8 CAV on the right side, with the troop code on the left (eg. HHC 21).

The Spinning-Vee with the squadron code was usually repeated on the rear hatch, usually in the centre of the left oval door panel.

Plate D: *Cross-sectional Drawing: M2A2 Bradley Infantry Fighting Vehicle, 3rd Armored Cavalry Brigade, XVIII Airborne Corps, Iraq, February 1991*

Although the M2A2 IFV (and the comparable M3A2 CFV) are most easily distinguished by their exterior applique armour, both vehicles also had internal stowage changes compared to earlier versions. These changes were brought about due to live-fire trials; they were intended to reduce the probability of internal fires if the vehicle was hit by moving vulnerable ammunition to positions less likely to be struck. Unlike US Army tank interiors which are finished in gloss white, infantry vehicle interiors are finished in overall FS 24410 Green, a semi-gloss light green. This includes the turret interior as well. Surfaces that are exposed to the outside such as hatches are finished in the exterior colour, Forest Green. Working components or stowage items are in a variety of colours.

Plate E: *M270 MLRS, Battery A, 13th Field Artillery, 24th Infantry Division (Mechanised), Operation 'Desert Shield', Saudi Arabia, January 1991*
A single MLRS battery was attached to the divisional artillery (DIVARTY) of the 24th Infantry Division and was used mainly to support the division cavalry squadron during the fighting; another battery of MLRS was also provided from the attached 3/27th Field Artillery, 212th Field Artillery Brigade. This view shows the markings of the vehicle prior to the initiation of hostilities, at which point, the upward pointing Allied recognition chevron was added. The V designs, as mentioned earlier, were divisional insignia recalling the 'Victory' Division name. This particular vehicle has been named *Strictly Business* and the name is carried on the rocket launcher side and on the front of the armoured cab. The stencilling in the centre of the cab front is the new pattern unit code number (WAQBAA 00021). Other MLRS in the battalion were *Sudden Death* (A-11) and *Bone Crusher* (A-23). The bumper codes in black are in the standard position and are 24 13F A-13, and are repeated on the rear as well. The rocket pods themselves were finished in overall Forest Green.

Plate F1: *M270 MLRS, Battery C, 4th Battalion, 27th Field Artillery (MLRS), 2nd Armored Cavalry Regiment, Saudi Arabia, February 1991*
The 27th Field Artillery's three batteries were divided during the fighting, with C Battery supporting the 2nd Armoured Cavalry Regiment, and Batteries A and B remaining under the 75th Field Artillery Brigade. The brigade started the war as a corps asset of the 7th Jayhawks Corps, but after the initial salvoes, was attached to the 1st Armoured Division for the manoeuvre mission. This is an MLRS of Battery C, the tactical codes identify the battery: 61= Alpha Battery; 62 = Bravo Battery; 63= Charlie Battery. This unit adopted a scorpion with a MLRS rocket as its stinger as a unit insignia. The bumper codes for the battery were 4F27 C11, etc.

Plate F2: *M270 MLRS, Battery B, US Army Field Artillery Regiment (MLRS), Iraq, February 1991*
This colourfully marked MLRS served with an unidentified US Army field artillery battalion during 'Desert Storm'. The vehicle name *Bastogne* suggests it served with a Battery B, although the practice of naming vehicles beginning with the battery letter was not universal during 'Desert Storm'. The name is painted on a slightly darker background colour, probably caused when the name was masked during vehicle repainting.

Plate G: *M2A1 Bradley Infantry Fighting Vehicle, Common NATO Camouflage Scheme, 1987-1995*
In the mid-1980s, discussions took place in NATO to adopt a common camouflage scheme, finally agreeing on a German-designed system using three colours: FS 30051 Green, FS 34094 Brown and FS 37030 Black. This pattern began to be adopted in 1987 by the US Army, and the camouflage pattern was applied to new vehicles at the factory in San Jose. Older vehicles were gradually refinished in the pattern during major maintenance, though many vehicles retained the earlier monotone Forest Green pattern for many years, some up to the present. Because it was intended to be factory applied, the pattern tends to be more regular than past camouflage schemes. The illustrations here show the official pattern as applied to the Bradley vehicles. When fresh, brown tends to be a chocolate brown, but fades out in the sun.

INDEX

(References to illustrations are shown in **bold**. Plates are shown with page and caption locators in brackets.)

1st Armored Division 34
1st Cavalry Division **20**, 34, **35**, 41, **C** (46)
1st Infantry Division 33
2nd Armored Cavalry Brigade **21**, 34
2nd Armored Cavalry Regiment **F1** (47)
2nd Armored Division 15, **17**, **19**, 38
3rd Armored Cavalry Brigade 34, **D** (46–47)
3rd Armored Cavalry Regiment **A2** (46)
3rd Armored Division 33, 37
3rd Infantry Division 15
24th Infantry Division **24**, **33**, 33, **36**, **43**, 46, **A1** (46), **B** (46), **E** (47)

access 8, 18, **19**
ammunition 19, 21–22, 34, 37
ammunition stowage **12**, **15**, **16**, 17, 18, 33
amphibious capability **9**, 19
AMX-10 11
armament 3, 4, 39, **39**–40, **40**
    Firing Port Weapons **11**, 17–18
    M242 25mm Bushmaster cannon **9**, 18, 8–19, 21, 36, 37
    machine guns 18, 37
    Stinger missiles 41, **42**
    TOW anti-tank missile launcher **6**, 8, 14, 18, 19, 20, 22, 23, 36–37, 38
armour 6, 9–10, 13, 14, 15, 19–20, 22, 23–24, **24**, 33, **34**, 38
armoured infantry vehicles 3; 4–5
Armoured Personnel Carriers (APCs) 3, 5, 6, 8
    psychological effects on infantry 7–8
Armoured Reconnaissance Scout Vehicles (ARSVs) 5, 10–11, 38

BMP Infantry Combat Vehicle, the 4–5, 8, 11, 18, 21, 21–23, 38
British forces 3, 43, 44
bumper codes **C** (46), **E** (47), **F1** (47)

cancelled development programmes 10–11
Casey, Major-General George 8
chemical defence system 23
colour schemes **7**, **17**, **36**, 45, 46, **A–G** (46–47)
combat potential 22–23, 23(table)
commander, the **9**, **12**
costs 5, 13
crew 5, 14, 20–21
criticisms 15

'Desert Storm', Operation 22, 33–34, **35**, **36**, 36–39, **37**, 42, 44–45, **A–F** (46–47)
development 14
digital data handling system 39
driver, the 17

electro-optical dazzlers 37–38
Elevated Target Acquisition System (ETAS) 42–43

engine 17, 33
exports 33, 43–44

firing ports 8, **10**, **13**, 24
FMC Corporation 9, 10
foreign alternatives 11
FV.432: 3

General Electric 14
German forces 3, 4–5, 43, 44; *see also* Marder Infantry Combat Vehicle

heavy infantry vehicles 11, 13–14
High Survivability Version (HSV) 23–24, **24**
HS.30: 3

Improved Bradley Acquisition System (IBAS) 39
infantry squads 4–5, 7–8, 14, 20–21, **33**, 38–39
Integrated Sight Unit (ISU) 18, 22
internal layout **9**, **12**, **13**, **14**, **15**, 15, 17, **D** (46–47)

Larkin Task Force, the 11, 14
laser blinding weapons **36**, 38, 41–2, **42**
Lockheed 10

M1 Abrams tank 9, 33, 34, 36, 38
M2 Bradley IFV **7**, **9**, **10**, **12**, **13**, 14, 15, **17**, 17–19, **18**, 20, 23, 33–34
    A1: **21**, **23**, 23, **37**, **B** (46), **G** (47)
    A2: **14**, 23–24, **24**, **33**, 33, **34**, **35**, 39, **D** (46–47)
    comparison with BMP 21–23
    scale drawings **16**, **21**, **23**, **33**, **39**
M3 Bradley CFV **10**, 14–15, **15**, **16**, 17, 19–20, **20**, 23, 34
    A1 **A1** (46), **22**, 23, **36**, **C** (46)
    A2 **A2** (46), 23–24
M113 Armoured Cavalry Vehicle (ACAV) 6
M113 Armoured Personnel Carrier 3, 3–4, 5, 5–6, 8–9, 20
M800 ARSV 38
M901 ITV tank destroyers 20
Marder Infantry Combat Vehicle 4–5, 9, 11, 18
markings **17**, 45, **A–G** (46–47)
Medina Ridge, action at 37
MICV-65 (Mechanized Infantry Combat Vehicle) **3**, 5, 8–10
MICV/ARSV requirement harmonisation 11, 13–14
mines, threat of 6, 7
modifications 23–24, 33, 39
multiple rocket launcher vehicle, M270 MLRS **43**, 43, 43–45, **44**, **E** (47), **F** (47)

name 14–15
NATO, Common Camouflage Scheme 45, 46, **G** (47)

'Norfolk, Battle of' 38
organisation 20–21, 34

Pacific Car and Foundry Company 5
production 14, 24 (table), 33

Reforger exercise **18**
Royal Saudi Arabian Army 33

scout units 38
skirts **20**
smoke dischargers 18
Soviet Red Army 3, 4–5, 8, 11; *see also* BMP Infantry Combat Vehicle, the
speed 34, 36
squad leader, the 18
steering system 17
stowage 22, 23

tactics 3–4, 5, 5–6, 38–39
thermal imaging night sights 36
Training and Doctrine Command (TRADOC) 10, 11
transmission 14, 36
troop compartment **9**, **13**, **14**, **15**, **16**, 18
turret, the **6**, **12**, 14, 18

US Army Field Artillery Regiment **F2** (47)

variants
    ADATS **40**, 40
    Bradley FIST (Fire Support Team) **41**, 41
    Bradley Stinger Fighting Vehicle 40–41, **42**
    COMVAT (Combat Vehicle Armament Technology) 39–40, **40**
    ETAS (Elevated Target Acquisition System) 42–43
    LOSAT (Line-Of-Sight-Anti-Tank) **42**, 42
    M270 MLRS multiple rocket launcher vehicle 43–45, **44**, **E** (47), **F** (47)
    M987 Fighting Vehicle System (FVS) 43
    M1070 Electronic Fighting Vehicle System (EFVS) 43
    Stingray **36**, 38, 41–42, **42**
Vehicle Integrated Defense System 39
Vietnam War, the 5–6, 10
VLQ-8 missile countermeasure device 39

XM2 Infantry Fighting Vehicle (IFV) **6**, 14
XM3 Cavalry Fighting Vehicle (CFV) 14
XM701 MICV-65 **3**, 5, 10
XM723 MICV (Mechanized Infantry Combat Vehicle) **4**, 9–10, 14
XM734 6
XM765 AIFV (Armoured Infantry Fighting Vehicle) 9
XM800 ARSV 5, 10–11